The Danger of Not Reforming Known Evils, and Other Works
by William Williams
With chapters by C. Matthew McMahon

Copyright Information

The Danger of Not Reforming Known Evils, and Other Works by William Williams with chapters by C. Matthew McMahon
Edited by Therese B. McMahon

Copyright ©2022 by Puritan Publications and A Puritan's Mind™

Some language and grammar have been updated from the original manuscript. Any change in wording or punctuation has not changed the intent or meaning of the original authors, and has been made to aid the modern reader.

Published by Puritan Publications
A Ministry of A Puritan's Mind™ in Crossville, TN.
www.apuritansmind.com
www.puritanpublications.com

All rights reserved. No part of this publication may be reproduced, stored in a retrieval system or transmitted in any form by any means, electronic, mechanical, photocopy, recording or otherwise, without the prior permission of the publisher, except as provided by USA copyright law.

This Print Edition, 2022
Electronic Edition, 2022
Manufactured in the United States of America

ISBN: 978-1-62663-435-0
eISBN: 978-1-62663-434-3

Table of Contents

The Effectual and Outward Call 4

Meet William Williams 11

The Danger of Not Reforming Known Evils *The Inexcusableness of a Knowing People Refusing to be Reformed* 12

The Great Salvation Revealed and Offered in the Gospel Explained *and a Hearty Acceptance of it Urged* 38

    Outline of the Sermons 38

    To The Reader 42

    Part 1 47

    Part 2 73

    Part 3 91

    Part 4 116

    Part 5 137

The Serious Consideration that God Will Visit and Judge Men for Sin 167

Other Newly Published Works at Puritan Publications 186

The Effectual and Outward Call
by C. Matthew McMahon Ph.D., Th.D.

The Scriptures distinguish between the effectual call of God *through* the Gospel by the Spirit, and the *external* call of the Gospel addressed *in* the Word of God to all to whom that word is made known which hear it or read it. The *external* call includes a *declaration* of the plan of salvation and the promise of God to save all who consent to the terms of that plan. It is given as a command, exhortation and invitation to all who believe by faith the mercy proclaimed. There are also reasons given which should press men to repent and believe the Gospel to escape from the wrath to come. "For whosoever shall call upon the name of the Lord shall be saved," (Rom. 10:13). This external call is universal in the sense that it is addressed to all men indiscriminately to whom the gospel is sent. It is not confined to an age, nation, or class of men. The external call of the gospel is addressed to *all* men. God is *ready* to save. David says in Psalm 86:5, "Thou, Lord, art good, and ready to forgive; and plenteous in mercy unto all them that call upon thee." The prophet Isaiah in 55:1 gives the same sentiments when he writes, "Ho, every one that thirsteth, come ye to the waters, and he that hath no money; come ye, buy and eat; yea, come, buy wine and milk without money, and without price." Jesus Christ calls men *indiscriminately*, "Come unto me, all ye that labour and are heavy laden, and I will give you rest," (Matt. 11:28). All who labor, all who are heavy laden, all should come to him.[1] This external call is not inconsistent with the doctrine of predestination since predestination concerns only the purpose of God to render effectual, in particular cases, the call addressed to all men. The external call is the means by which the Spirit of God will regenerate and change a heart *through* the preaching of the Word of God.

Efficacious grace, or the effectual call of the Gospel, demonstrates the power of the Spirit of God instituting an efficacious influence upon all those who have been given to the Son as his inheritance. Such grace and work are not hypothetical, but effectual to render the subject changed and converted. This work is the exercise of "the mighty power of God," who speaks *change* into existence. The 1647 Westminster Confession of Faith says, "All those whom God hath predestinated unto life, and those only, He is pleased, in his appointed and accepted time, effectually to call, by his Word and Spirit, out of that state of sin and death in which they are by nature, to grace and salvation by Jesus Christ; enlightening their minds, spiritually and savingly, to understand the things of God, taking away their heart of stone, and giving unto them a heart of flesh; renewing their wills, and by his almighty power determining them to that which is good; and effectually drawing them to Jesus Christ; yet so as they come most freely, being made willing by his

---

[1] It is true that those who "labor" and are "heavy laden" have the Spirit of God working on them. All "thirsty" sinners are to come. But the call to them is still indiscriminate because the preacher does not know who is thirsty, who is laboring, or who are heavy laden. Only *God* knows that.

grace," (WCF 10:1). In this way efficacious grace is irresistible and immediate as *God* intends. Typically, the explanation of this efficacious call and work upon the soul is taught in the scriptural term *regeneration*. Titus 3:5 states, "...Not by works of righteousness which we have done, but according to his mercy he saved us, by the washing of regeneration, and renewing of the Holy Ghost."

Regeneration is the Spirit's sovereign work of taking a depraved soul and infusing into it the life-giving spiritual power of holy change. It is the supernatural act of God where a new and divine life is infused into the elect person who is spiritually dead and made spiritually alive. The soul in this case is passive in that it is the object to be affected by the Spirit. *Regeneration* is the effect of almighty power as much as the opening the eyes of the blind or the unstopping by a word the ears of the deaf. It is instantaneous and an act of *sovereign grace*. The Apostle John says in John 1:12-13, "But to all who did receive him, who believed in his name, he gave the right to become children of God, who were born, not of blood nor of the will of the flesh nor of the will of man, but of God (*cf.* John 5:26; James 1:18; 2 Peter 1:4). Regeneration is given life through the seed which is planted in the soul – that seed is the word of God. Peter instructs us in 1 Peter 1:23, "...since you have been born again, not of perishable seed but of imperishable, through the living and abiding word of God."[2]

---

[2] This seed does not always operate in the same manner (as is clear in the case of infants). Sometimes God regenerates infants (or those incapable of rational thought such as someone autistic or handicapped)

The Bible teaches us that from Christ the whole church body derives all its supplies by which it lives and grows from this regenerating power and life that is infused by Christ's Spirit. "Because I live, ye shall live also," (John 14:19). "I am the resurrection, and the life," (John 11:25). "I am that bread of life," (John 6:48). "He that eateth my flesh, and drinketh my blood, dwelleth in me and I in him," (John 6:56). "This is that bread which came down from heaven...he that eateth of this bread shall live forever," (John 6:58). "We shall be saved by his life," (Rom. 5:10). "As the Father hath life in himself, so hath he given to the Son to have life in himself," (John 5:26). "Thou hast given him power over all flesh, that he should give eternal life to as many as thou hast given him," (John 17:2). Believers are the children of God as the subjects of a *new birth*, which is the teaching of Christ on *regeneration*. The subjects of regeneration are born of God and born of the Spirit. They are begotten of God. "That which is born of the flesh, is flesh; and that which is born of the Spirit, is spirit," (John 3:6). These are, "born, not of blood, nor of the will of the flesh, nor of the will of man, but of God," (John 1:13). Even as the Apostle Peter states in 1 Peter 1:23, "Being born again, not of corruptible seed, but of incorruptible, by the Word of God, which liveth and abideth forever."

This same regenerating power is seen throughout the entire Bible functioning in the same way, both in the Old

---

via the power of the Spirit through the Word in some other means that he has kept secret; but nonetheless is still effectual by the word of God applied to a person, and instills the seed of faith.

Testament and New Testament. Sinners are saved in the same manner in every administration of the *Covenant of Grace*. In Deuteronomy 30:6 Moses says, "The Lord thy God will circumcise thine heart, and the heart of thy seed, to love the Lord thy God with all thine heart, and with all thy soul, that thou mayest live." In Ezekiel 11:19 it is said, "I will give them one heart, and I will put a new spirit within you; and I will take the stony heart out of their flesh, and will give them an heart of flesh." In Ezekiel 36:26 it is written, "A new heart also will I give you, and a new spirit will I put within you: and I will take away the stony heart out of your flesh, and I will give you an heart of flesh. And I will put my Spirit within you, and cause you to walk in my statutes, and ye shall keep my judgments and do them." Jeremiah 24:7 is explicit, "I will give them a heart to know me." The indwelling Spirit or Christ dwelling in us is the principle and source of that new life of which the believer is made the subject. This is what is called *the beginning of new life*.

I make mention of the differentiation between the *outward* call and the *effectual* call because all three of William Williams pieces in this work set themselves squarely inside understanding the difference between the two. Without having a clear delineation between the Gospel preached, and the Gospel applied, some of his thoughts will seem out of place. But rest assured, they are not.

Williams' first piece on The Danger of Not Reforming Known Evils, is a master-exhortation in calling the wayward *church*, those professing they have been effectually called, to reform those things in their midst that need correcting.

People who have been changed by the Spirit *desire* holiness. Worldly Christians like the "idea" of holiness, but they have other hobbies they would rather attend to. If the people of Christ's church are inwardly changed, why would they not want to change and reform those things that are amiss among them? In such people there would be a great inexcusableness to them for being a *knowing people* and yet refusing to be reformed. And if they do not *see* that they have need of reforming those things that are amiss, what does that say about them? Or, even worse, what if they *do not want* to change those things that are known evils? Or run away from a sound ministry in order to avoid them altogether? This argues their *desperate* state, even though they may outwardly be *professing* believers.

    William's second piece is on the great salvation that is offered in the Gospel. He sets this down in five main propositions to show the Gospel's greatness, as well as the means and manner in which sinners may come to attain the salvation offered in the Gospel by Jesus Christ. This particularly applies to the idea of the outward call which is indiscriminate, and the inward call of the Spirit in the heart which is particular. His main text is, "How shall we escape, if we neglect so great salvation," (Hebrews. 2:3). He teaches the main doctrine that salvation revealed and offered in the Gospel is great and glorious, and the neglect of it will bring upon men great and unavoidable misery.

    His third piece is to prompt a *serious consideration* that God through Christ will visit and judge all men for their sin, taken from Job 31:14, "What then shall I do when God rises up? and when he visits, what shall I answer him?" Here he outlines the reality that though the Gospel is preached among the nations, and men hear it, what good will it do them if they do not receive it and heed its call? What will they do when God rises up against them at judgment? And if they neglect the Gospel, God's only means of escaping the wrath to come, they will find themselves at their mortal end standing before a holy Judge who will sentence them accordingly by his law, for their sins.

Williams is an *excellent* preacher, (how we ought to desire more like him today), and yet, he has a grand pastoral heart, delivering powerful messages that are fitting to be heard by those in and out of the watered down church in our day and age. May you be blessed in your endeavors in hearing and heeding his relevant messages in glorification of the Gospel of Jesus Christ, changing those things that are amiss, holding steadfastly to the Gospel, and looking forward to the day in which you will stand before God in the righteousness of Jesus Christ.

In His Grace,
C. Matthew McMahon, Ph.D., Th.D.
From my study April, 2022
"...search the Scriptures..." (John 5:39).
www.apuritansmind.com
www.puritanpublications.com
www.gracechapeltn.com

Meet William Williams
by C. Matthew McMahon, Ph.D., Th.D.

There is not much known about William Williams (1666-1741). He was a colonial minister who graduated from Harvard in 1683 at the age of 18. He settled in Hatfield, MA in 1685, and married Elizabeth, daughter of Rev. John Cotton, July 8, 1686. Later, after his wife's death, he married Christian Stoddard (of the famous Stoddards). As for children, (by first marriage), he had William Williams Jr., Elisha Williams, Martha Williams Partridge, and an infant daughter that died. Children (by his second marriage) were Solomon Williams, Israel Williams, Elizabeth Williams Barnard, and Dorothy Williams.

He ministered in Hatfield, being part of their congregation beginning at age 21.

Williams was buried in Hill Cemetery in Hatfield. His funeral sermon was preached by his second wife's nephew, the celebrated Jonathan Edwards (1703-1758), minister at Northampton, who later became President of Princeton.

The Danger of Not Reforming Known Evils

The Inexcusableness of a Knowing People Refusing to be Reformed

1 Samuel 3:13, "For I have told him, that I will judge his house for ever, for the iniquity which he knoweth: because his sons made themselves vile, and he restrained them not."

God's people are not exempt from judgment. For those who are truly godly and dear to God, if by their sinful behavior they dishonor God and religion, they open themselves up to being humbled by God here in this world, even though their sin is forgiven and shall not condemn them in the other world. It is necessary for the vindication of God's name and the promoting of their own good to give some public testimony of his displeasure against sin.

Not only those who are of a profane and vicious spirit, but also the sins of those who are upright and sincere help to bring public rebukes and judgments on themselves and others. God was so displeased with the impatience and hesitancy of Moses and Aaron that he did not allow them to enter Canaan (Deut. 32:51-52). God was so offended with David in the matter of Uriah that he brought a great deal of sorrow upon his family and kingdom. He was so provoked with Solomon for the idolatry of his many wives that he tore away ten parts of the kingdom of Israel out of the hand of his son. And God denounces an awful threatening against the house of Eli for his undue toleration of and responsibility for the wickedness of his sons. Such examples should instruct us to maintain a reverent fear of God and his opinion of sin. We should not think ourselves exempt from his punishment because of our relation to God, but to maintain a holy awe and trembling in our hearts because of his holiness and jealousy, he who is of purer eyes than to look upon sin.

In our text we may notice three things. 1. A severe threatening denounced against the house of Eli, "I have told him," by the message before sent to him, "that I will judge." The word 'judge' signifies to condemn, punish, or destroy. Here it seems to indicate 'to punish.'

"His house," that is, his family or posterity, which is often called a man's house.

"Forever," that is, either until they are utterly wasted and consumed, or rather for a long time, as the word *forever* is often used. This was in part fulfilled when his two sons were slain by the Philistines (1 Sam. 4:11), in part when Saul slew Ahimelech and his family (1 Sam. 22:18), and finally when the priesthood was transferred from the house of Eli and Ithamar to that of Eliezer by Solomon about eighty years after (1 Kings 2:27).

2. The reason for this threatening is because his sons made themselves vile, and he did not restrain them. Their sin was very horrid and remarkable, as is reported in the preceding chapter. Their sins rendered them abominable to God and contemptible to the people. They brought their sacred offices and God's holy ordinances into contempt. Yet their father did not use the authority which God had given him as a high priest, as a judge or chief magistrate, in

punishing them, as by the Law of God he was obliged to do. But was content himself to give them an easy and gentle reproof.

3. The aggravation of this sin, which is especially taken notice of as the immediate cause of the judgment, was his son's iniquity which he knew about. He could not plead ignorant for lack of evidence, for the cry of their wickedness went all over Israel. And God had particularly warned him of it by a messenger sent to him (1 Sam. 2:27 and following). Further, the matter was so notorious that his parental fondness and indulgence of his sons seemed to have clouded his judgment in punishing them suitable to their guilt.

That is the clause in the text that I would particularly take notice of at this time, and from it you may take this *doctrine*.

DOCTRINE. It is highly offensive to God and shows men to be at risk of God's judgment when they will not reform what they know to be amiss.

The fact that Eli knew his sons to be vile and yet he did not do what he should have to restrain them aggravated his own sin. *Sometimes* people, through ignorance, are at a disadvantage to know the mind of God in particular cases. Or maybe the matter is disputable. It's a question to them whether the thing is a sin or not. Now though this doesn't wholly excuse sin, it may lessen its severity.

But when men have sufficient light to expose sin, and even though they confess it they persist in it, this makes them very guilty before God and shows their offence to be very great. It is here that God threatens in a peculiar manner to punish his own people, as in Amos 3:2, "You only have I known of all the families of the earth, therefore will I punish you for all your iniquities." Why is this? Not because God loves them less than he does others, but because his name and honor suffer by *their* sins. Because they continue in sin when they have greater light than others that still wander in darkness, they are more inexcusable (Job 15:22). Also, as James 4:17 states, "To him that knows to do good and does it not, to him it is sin."

I shall first give you the confirmation of the doctrine, and then make some application of it.

1. Such behavior discovers a prevailing love for sin. It shows that sin has a great deal of power in their hearts, for the more light that is resisted in sinning, the stronger and deeper love men have to it. Their pleas and excuses for it, as well as their willingness to justify it, show that it has primacy in their affections, and this corrupts and blinds their judgments.

Were there sufficient hatred of sin as there ought to be, the heart would show a greater resistance of it, would shun temptations when they appear, and would make great effort to mortify it. But man's eagerness in serving it despite sufficient light and conviction is a sign it has a great deal of power over them. This reason the apostle gives us for why Balaam was so set to curse Israel in 2 Peter 2:5 was because "He loved the wages of unrighteousness." To love sin is a bad sign. Where it reigns, it shows a man's state to be bad. The psalmist gives it as the character of a wicked man in Psalm 52:3, "You love evil more than good." When men prefer sin before holiness in their ordinary habitual course, it shows them to be in a bad state. It shows the heart to be lacking in the exercise of grace which ought to be maintained. Now love for sin very much aggravates sin. John 3:19 says, "This is the condemnation that light is come into the world, and men love darkness rather than light."

2. It shows a lack of love to God; too little sense of and regard for God's honor. Sin is loathsome and abominable to God. He looks on it with displeasure and abhorrence, and it should also be seen that way by us and be the object of our hatred and displeasure. And where a spirit of love to God is exercised, it will be that way. They that love the Lord will hate evil, and so the psalmist expresses his indignation against sin, Psalm 101:3, "I hate the works of such as turn aside, it shall not cleave to me." And Psalm 119:104, "I hate every false way."

If a person has a tender respect for God's glory, his name and honor is dear to them. This will make them afraid of provoking him, of doing anything that will lessen and obscure it; and make them watchful against all encroachments of sin. They will be ready to say as Joseph did in Genesis 39:9, "How can I do this great wickedness and sin against God?" When people persevere in the practice of known evils, it shows either a lack of love for God or the lack of the exercise of love to God. For if love for God were being exercised, sin would be a burden and a grief to the soul. Holiness would be desired and sought after with all possible means (John 14:23). Now this will be readily granted, that men are very much to blame either when they lack a spirit of love to God, or don't maintain it in a lively exercise and practice. God is worthy of our love; our best affections are due him, both because of his infinite perfections and his innumerable benefits. The other reason is because this is the foundation of all evangelical obedience.

3. It is an argument of spiritual deadness, stupidity, and dullness of conscience that sin can be left alone and suffered to lie quietly in the heart. A tender conscience may be sometimes clouded with ignorance, and through mistakes pass a wrong judgment in some cases, allowing one to remain for a time in some sin without repentance. But otherwise, a tender conscience will rebuke and condemn sin. It is God's deputy in the soul and will witness for him when his honor is condemned, and his law violated. When David merely cut off the skirt of Saul's robe, his heart "smote him," (1 Sam. 24:5). When Peter remembered the words of Christ, "he went out and wept bitterly," (Matt. 26:75). A sensible conscience will fill the soul with accusations, making it uneasy under the burden of its own guilt and restlessness to be delivered from it. When the Apostle Paul had stirred up the consciences of the Corinthian Christians to reflect on their sinful involvement regarding the person among who was exhibiting a prideful spirit, you see how it worked in them (2 Cor. 7:11). They could have no rest until they were thoroughly clear of it and had by genuine repentance testified their displeasure against it. It is every Christian's unquestionable duty to get and keep a tender conscience. The lack of a due sense of God's unspotted holiness and purity, and the certainty of his righteous

judgment results in a lack of concern to please God and prove their love for him by a holy life. Yes, if conscience is allowed to fall asleep, the soul lies like a town unguarded, ready to become prey to an approaching enemy. Satan easily gets an advantage over such a person, and many *saddening* breaches are made in the peace of their souls.

4. Because it shows a greater choice and freedom in sinning. Such people do not sin because of the sudden surprise of temptation; they sin with more deliberation. Now the more freely men commit sin, and the greater the consent of the will there is in it, the more vile it is. It reveals a very bad state or frame of heart when men have lost the sense of God's authority and the awe of his judgment. And therefore, such sins are the more heinous and offensive to God. John 15:22 says, "If I had not come and spoken to them, they had had no sin, but now they have no cloak for their sin." The amount of light they possessed made their sin inexcusable and took away all pleas and pretenses they previously had to excuse or cover it. They can't say they did not know it was sin, or that it was a thing so offensive to God or dangerous to themselves. Possessing the *light* of the gospel shows these things to them. Christ tells us that such sins expose a person to greater judgment (Luke 12:47). The servant that knew his Lord's will, and did not prepare himself to do according to that will, shall be beaten with many stripes. And hereafter it exposes to a worse condemnation. So, when the conscience of a sinner is awakened, the remembrance of the Light that has been resisted, as well as the warnings and convictions that have

been slighted, makes deep wounds in the conscience, causing fears and agonies in the spirit.

    5. It also shows there is little dread in their hearts for God's judgments. Sin exposes men to the just displeasure of a holy and righteous God. So often by his providences he reveals his wrath against the ungodliness and unrighteousness of men, expecting that these events should be a means to restrain them from continuing any longer in their impenitence. But even when his wrath is not made visible in the punishment of sin, it is shown in his threatening against it, hanging like a flaming sword over the head of a sinner. This should be enough to make them afraid of exposing themselves to divine justice, like David said in Psalm 119:120, "My flesh trembles for fear of thee, and I am afraid of thy judgments," and Job in Job 31:23, "Destruction from God was a terror to me, and by reason of his highness I could not endure." God requires men to "stand in awe and sin not," (Psa. 4:4). And Isaiah 26:9 says, "When his judgments are abroad in the earth, the inhabitants of the world will learn righteousness." Corrections should be instructive, we should learn the evil of sin by them, and be afraid of continuing in it. If there were any suitable awe of the justice, or truth of God on the heart, any sense of the terribleness of his displeasure and what a fearful thing it is to be the sorrowful subject of his threatenings or judgments, it would be so. Therefore, those whose hearts are glued to their lusts and idols and will not part with them will expose themselves to the wrath and jealously of a sin-revenging God. And though they have the light of truth concerning the

judgment of God in his threatenings and providences, they are not changed or restrained by it.

I move to the application.

USE 1. This shows us that those under the prevailing of an unreformed spirit are many times more culpable in the sight of God than they are aware. Not only are the evils they entertain very offensive to God, but the fact that they do *not improve* or correct their ways based on the light given them renders their sin very culpable in the sight of God. It is bad enough when God's people allow themselves to become corrupt and degenerate. But it is worse when they continue to do so and refuse to be reclaimed. They are to be blamed on a double account.

1. With respect to their ingratitude for the light that is given them. Their unwillingness to submit to it shows their low esteem of it. They don't acknowledge the mercy of God in it. God frowns on his people when he lets them alone in their sins, without using the means that are proper to convince, reform, convert, and bring them back to their duty. When he allows them to walk in their own ways, as he did the Gentile world (Acts 14:6), and when he lets them alone (Hosea 4:17). When he leaves them to blindness and darkness and doesn't show them their sin or danger nor call them to repentance, it is a sign God has marked them out for his vengeance and displeasure.

But on the other hand, it is a great mercy and blessing when God takes pains with men to bring them to a sight of sin and a conviction of their duty, when he reveals his will to them, shows them how they should govern themselves and order their life, testifies against their evils, warns them of the danger of sin, and encourages them to obedience by promises of mercy. These are his means to work on a heart and gain men to their duty. As Psalm 147:19 says, "He gave his statutes to Jacob and his judgments to Israel," *etc.* And as a result, when Israel disregards these, God is not pleased. And Hosea 8:12 says, "I have written to them the great things of my law, but they were counted as a strange thing," or a *foreign thing*, as a thing they had no concern with, not belonging to them, and something they did not desire to be governed by. Whatever pretenses men make of being thankful for the word of God, when they speak of having light and grace as a privilege while not yielding themselves to the obedience to the light nor conforming themselves to the commands of it, they are not truly thankful at all (Neh. 9:26).

2. An unwillingness to be reformed argues for a hopeless spirit. It shows their hearts are set upon their evil ways. As in Hosea 11:7, "My people are bent to backsliding from me: though they called them to the most High, none at all would exalt him." Like the depth of a disease when it resists healing medicines, when suitable means are used to bring people to repentance and yet all prove to be ineffectual, it shows them to be irredeemable. They say, either in words or practices, as those in Jeremiah 44:16 said, "As for the word thou hast spoken to us in the name of the Lord, we will not hearken unto thee." When men withstand

God's means of conviction, when they don't hear or listen to the voice of God's warnings or judgments, when they plead for sin and are unwilling to repent, reform and turn to God genuinely, they are in a very bad state spiritually. It is bad enough when the hearts of a people have turned from God to their lusts. But it is worse when they will not return and prefer to continue in their evil ways.

USE 2. This is to warn you not to resist the light that shows your sin and brings you to your duty. It is a dangerous thing to neglect to reform what you know to be amiss as it exposes those who are guilty of it to many judgments. Eli had been forewarned of the wickedness of his sons. But his sinful indulgence towards them blinded him. And here God tells him, he will judge *his house forever*. So the prophet declares against Amaziah in 2 Chron. 25:16, "I know God has determined to destroy thee, because thou hast done this, and hast not hearkened to my counsel." Notwithstanding sufficient testimonies from God, men do sometimes harden their hearts. And by persisting in sin, they expose themselves to spiritual, temporal, and eternal judgments. I will remind you of some of the ways by which people sometimes do it, that you may be cautioned against them.

1. By pleading the example of others. Bad examples are very destructive and provide an opportunity to further harden men in sin. Jeroboam's idolatry had a fatal influence on all the succeeding kings of Israel. As you find in Jeremiah 44:17, they justified themselves in their idolatrous practices from the example of their kings, princes, and fathers before them. But this is no sufficient vindication. If the thing in its

nature or under such circumstances is evil, the practice of others will not make it good, no matter who or how many they are. You know that good men have their failings. And besides, all are not good that are assumed to be so. Many that the world calls wise, knowing men are and will be found to be fools at last. But if they are never so good or wise, you must follow no one any further than they follow Christ (1 Cor. 11:1). Precepts must be your rule, not examples (Isa. 8:20). There is hardly any duty that someone or another does not fail in, or any sin but some have fallen into. Laziness, both to principles and practices, often prevails among a people. So that if you make this a rule, you will find very little to be reformed. And yes, a great part of Scripture must be put aside as useless and unnecessary.

    2. By entertaining biases against those that warn of God's judgment as if they did it because of some ill will. This was one reason God's people rejected the word God sent by the prophet Jeremiah (Jer. 43:2), "The Lord hath not sent thee, but Baruch the Son of Neriah set thee on." Also, Jeremiah 6:10, "The word of the Lord is unto them a reproach." They interpret faithful reproofs to be reproaches, they say they are railed on. Ahab was prejudiced against Elijah and Micaiah, as if their reproofs were coming from a lack of love to him. Sometimes people pretend that others would keep them from enjoying their liberties, or they don't know the circumstances of their condition. Or that sometimes that they just want to target their own particular interest. But these pretenses are ordinarily from the deceitfulness of sin, or the efforts of Satan to harden the

heart; there is no just reason for them. Our duty, when reproved, is seriously to examine the case. If the word of God condemns the practice, that is sufficient to deter us from it. For it is by this that God will either justify or condemn us.

3. By trusting their religious privileges or seeming goodness in other cases. The carnal Jews when reproved for their oppression, injustice, and idolatry and called to amend their ways, boasted of their privileges. Jeremiah 7:4 says, "The temple of the Lord are these," as if their visible relation to God and external observations would secure them from judgments and in doing so, making this a cloak for wickedness as in Prov. 7:14, "I have peace-offerings with me, this day I have performed my vows." In this way carnal Christians rest on their external acts of devotion. They think that because they attend the worship of God in public, pray with their families and the like, that God will excuse their immorality. They trust in their righteousness and commit iniquity (Ezek. 33:13). But these things aggravate rather than excuse sin. God calls for universal obedience; the doing of one duty will not compensate for the neglect of another (James 2:11). Herod did many things, and heard John gladly, but would not part with his Herodias. The Pharisee could boast that he was no extortioner, no adulterer. But he could not say that he was not proud. God that calls you to pray, to hear, to meditate on his word also calls you to live soberly and righteously, to walk humbly with God. Partiality in religion spoils it and utterly excludes men of its rewards. James 1:26, "If a man seems to be religious, and bridles not his tongue, his religion is vain." If the heart is upright, all

duty will be chosen, and all sin avoided. Psalm 119:6 says, "Then shall I not be ashamed when I have respect to all thy commandments."

4. By presuming on the mercy of God, hoping that shall secure them from the strokes of justice. They sin freely and cry, "God is merciful." They don't think God will be so severe as he threatens, or that men would have them believe. Deuteronomy 29:19, "When he hears the words of this curse, that he bless himself, saying, 'I shall have peace, though I walk in the imagination of my heart.'" This hardens the hearts of a great many people. They take up wrong conceptions of God's mercy as if he were of so pitiful and tender a nature that he could not bear to see men suffer what he threatens. But you must know that God is just, as well as merciful; and it is not unmerciful for God to punish men according to his threatening. Yes, his truth and faithfulness oblige him to it. God has determined the way and time for the exercise of his mercy; and if these are neglected, no mercy will be shown. The very devils may as well hope for mercy as impenitent unbelievers who neglect in the day of salvation to seek for mercy. You cannot take a more direct and ready way to turn away the heart of a merciful God from you than by abusing his goodness to strengthen yourselves in rebellion against him. This is a most vile abuse of it and an unreasonable inference from it. Romans 6:1 states, "Shall we continue in sin, that grace may abound? God forbid!" It is a thought to be abhorred.

5. By entertaining purposes of future repentance. Men know their course is evil and such as God condemns.

They dare not justify the sinful practices which they indulge. But they still their consciences with this, that they intend to repent of it and be none the worse for it. They believe they can and will repent, and all shall be well. These plans for future repentance make them bold to continue in sin against all counsels and reproofs. But alas repentance is not so easy a work. The heart that is now so much in love with sin and so full of enmity to holiness will not easily be changed. A deceitful heart will find future excuses when those present ones are answered; the natural, sinful man will struggle hard before it is subdued. Not only that, but repentance is also a grace of God's giving; the heart of stone is too hard for any created power to break. And as it is what God gives, so it is what he gives freely (2 Tim. 2:25). Many that presume on having repentance at leisure find themselves disappointed; either a sudden death takes them, or a hard heart and a sleepy conscience creeps in and takes over. It is a bold adventure to reject God's gracious offers, presuming on future time or grace.

USE 3. Examine whether you are not faulty in this matter. Are there not several things which you know to be duties neglected; several things that you know to be sins practiced? We live in a land of light. We have great advantages to know the mind of God and to know how we should adorn the gospel and our profession of it. The grace of God toward us, both as to light and peace under gospel privileges, is very distinguishing. There may be errors in practice that arise through ignorance and inadvertency. And some points that are disputable that people are not aware of. Yet surely, the evils of this country are for the most part in such things as are known. It is not the lack of light, but the deficiency of accepting and submitting to the light that we have that handicaps the Reformation, which has been so long called for.

1. As to the duty of cultivating seasons and means of grace to a repentance from dead works by faith in the Lord Jesus Christ while the patience and longsuffering of God is continued. People that have been brought up under the call of the gospel and have had its duties so frequently instructed cannot be ignorant of these things. The word is plain concerning a present repentance and conversion to God. Isaiah 55:67 states, "Seek the Lord while he may be found, call upon him whilst he is near. Let the wicked forsake his way and the unrighteous man his thoughts," *etc.* And 2 Corinthians 6:1-2, "Behold now is the accepted time; now is the day of salvation," *etc.* How plainly Scripture warns of the danger of neglecting it! Hebrews 2:3 says, "How shall we escape, if we neglect so great salvation?" There will be no escaping or avoiding condemnation. God shows the riches of his grace in affording the seasons of grace to men. These are not to be slighted and trifled away but seriously, seasonably, and faithfully regarded. We cast a great dishonor upon Christ and show contempt of the love of God in the work of redemption when we disregard peace and reconciliation with him and when the fruits of redeeming love in sanctification and holiness are counted a burden instead of a privilege. It is a dishonorable and daring presumption, as well as disobedience, when God calls for

present repentance and conversion to defer the matter to some future time. Surely, men know it is their duty to put honor on the Lord Jesus Christ and to acknowledge him in his office of a Redeemer. Surely it is fit that he who has undergone such abasement and sufferings should be glorious in the eyes of those to whom he is offered, and the fruits of his redeeming love be received with all thankfulness. This is plainly required. John 5:23 says he will have all men "honor the Son as they honor the Father." And how is Christ honored, if he is not believed in and obeyed? (John 3:23; Heb. 5:9). Does not everyone confess that there is no other way of salvation, but this which God has consecrated through faith in his blood? Yet how many are there who neglect these great duties to live in unbelief? They do not honor the seasons of grace. They feel no misery in their estrangement from God, captivity to sin and Satan. They do not groan after redemption. They are more intent on securing the world than obtaining heaven. They are more preoccupied with what they shall eat and drink and what they will wear more than how they may glorify God, adorn themselves with the Gospel, and secure the happiness of their souls in Christ and their inheritance of that glory which he has purchased.

    2. As to the means of worship which God has appointed, whether public, private, or secret. Certainly, the omissions in them that are among us are not through ignorance. Men know and confess that God is the Supreme and first Being, the fountain of all goodness. And as such he is the proper object of worship as all mercies flow from him.

We should ask of him in prayer and acknowledge him with praise. As to the secret duties of worship, how plain is the precept in Matthew 6:6, "When you pray, enter into your closet, and when you have shut your door, pray to your Father who is in secret," *etc*. Every man has personal wants, sins, and temptations, as well as many concerns that are most fit to be transacted in secret between God and his own soul. Therefore, to omit this practice is both an act of disobedience to God and a great prejudice to yourselves. Yet are there not many who are strangers to this duty? They can seldom find time to converse with God in secret. They often sin in secret, but they don't pray in secret.

And as to the public worship of God, how plainly has God brought its separate parts together? And particularly, that very much neglected ordinance of the Lord's Supper, instructing all his disciples to do it in remembrance of him (Luke 22:19). In doing so, they keep up a thankful memorial of the death of Christ and its great ends. They rest their dependence on him for the blessings purchased by it. God having received such a full satisfaction, and the Covenant of Grace so fully confirmed on us, that love to Christ and hatred of sin might be increased and inflamed by the lively representation of his painful sufferings and bitter death. These things are so plain, yet how many live year after year in its neglect? Pretending to have a desire after it, they do not acknowledge God's authority in it. For if such motives came from a real esteem of it, from a real tenderness, they would set themselves to understand the nature, end, and use of it. They would want to reform their lives, crying day and night to God for his sanctifying grace to purify their hearts and fit them for communion with God in it. But how is this neglected? Such people will be without excuse in the day of Christ.

3. As to families, do men not know that it is their duty to educate and instruct their families in religion and virtue while restraining from impieties and immoralities? This is plain in Proverbs 22:6, "Train up a child in the way he should go," and Ephesians 6:4, "Bring them up in the nurture and admonition of the Lord." For this, Abraham is honored and commended by God. Genesis 18:19, "I know Abraham that he will command his children and household after him, and they shall keep the way of the Lord to do justice and judgment." Parents should be instruments to convey the best blessings to their children. Not only the ties of religion and conscience, but of nature as well. It will be gross hypocrisy in you to neglect their spiritual education, as well as a great unfaithfulness to God and to their souls. Have you not been the immediate instruments of propagating original sin to them? And should not this oblige you to do the best you can for them, that they may be delivered from its guilt? Besides, you have a special interest in them. You are always with them. You know their tempers and dispositions. You have peculiar advantages to be instilling the principles of piety and virtue in them, to season them to the practice of religion, civility, and industry. The great concern of upholding religion and propagating it to succeeding generations should be a pressing encouragement to this work. The work of Christ in our

towns and churches will soon diminish if this is neglected. They will be like unpolished stones, unfit to be laid in any building, if their virtuous and pious education is neglected. Eli's posterity was hurt for his indulgence. So was David's, though he was a very holy man. Therefore, those who know these things and yet neglect a godly education of their families, who indulge them in ignorance of things that are fundamental to their salvation and conversion are largely to blame. Whatever excuse may be made for such things among the heathen, those who profess to be Christians, who know their duty and have so many encouragements to do it and yet refuse to be reformed, have no excuse.

4. Do not men know that an inordinate affection to the things of this world is very unbecoming to those that profess Christianity, and is forbidden in the word of God? James 4:4, "Ye adulterers and adulteresses, know ye not that the friendship of the world is enmity with God," *etc.* Hebrews 13:5 says, "Let your conversation be without covetousness." (Matt. 6:19-20, 31-32). As Colossians 3:5 states, when one esteems and loves the world and replaces desires which are due to God with the world, this is idolatry. It is as idolatrous to embrace worldly things as it is to bow down to a stick or a stone. Men wrong their souls and wound their consciences when they take unrighteous gain, defraud, or oppress in their dealings, don't deal truly and honestly, or neglect paying their just debts or contributing to necessary acts of charity. These men dare not depend on divine providence or on the encouragement of the promises of God. When they begrudge God his due, and the poor their

due, they identify with the company of sinners. Their worldly cares take control of their time and their thoughts, choke convictions and hinder the duties of religion. Their care for the body crowds out care for the soul, and things of the world make them neglect heaven. How does such a spirit prevail, despite convictions and professions to the contrary?

5. Does not everyone know that intemperance is evil? The very light of nature condemns it. The word of God not only witnesses against gross intemperance such as drunkenness but all that tends toward it. And does not the gospel more especially require men to live soberly (Titus 2:12-13), to govern their appetites to food and drink, to not frequent bars or give way to an inordinate affection to strong drink? For these types of behaviors are evidence of a great abuse of light that has been afforded.

USE 4. Of Exhortation. Be persuaded then to reform those things that you know to be amiss and are plainly discovered to be sins. "Therefore, to him that knows to do good and does it not, to him it is sin," (James 4:17). If you neglect this, there will be just reason to fear that God's displeasure will not only continue but also increase. God is as angry with men's pride and stubbornness in contempt of his warnings as formerly he was. It is a dangerous thing for a people against whom God has a controversy to delay their repentance and continue in the causes of his anger. God limits his patience. He limits how long he will wait before his wrath breaks out, until there is no remedy. Our wisdom therefore is to take up the matter quickly, as in Numbers

16:49. We are to remove what we know is evil and to search out what we do not know. In particular,

1. Reform those things your own conscience tells you is amiss, those things that it condemns you for. Conscience is God's monitor in your heart, and you should listen to it (as you would to a messenger from heaven) when it warns you of evil committed or duty neglected. Are there not secret resolutions to avoid those evils or do those duties that conscience warns you about? Obey the voice of conscience in these things. Whatever it is that it witnesses to, don't ignore it. "A wounded spirit who can bear?" (Prov. 18:14).

2. Reform what you often confess to be amiss. How often are you lamenting and complaining about misspent time, the abuse of the seasons and right use of the means of grace, ingratitude for gospel mercies, the neglect of government over your spirits and passions, inordinate affection to the things of the world, and an indifference and coldness in the things of God's worship and your own salvation? How sad is it when a man's prayers serve only for a testimony of his hypocrisy! They show evidence of the deceitfulness of his heart in all the *religious acts* that he performs. If there were a hearty sorrow for such evils, and a due sense of them, it would be manifested in a serious endeavor to both reform and mortify them. Otherwise, it is merely hypocrisy.

3. Reform such things as are plainly witnessed against from the word of God. You confess the word of God to be the rule according to which your lives and actions should be ordered, your guide in matters of instituted

worship and moral duties: truth, justice, temperance, love, modesty, and the like. So be careful that you do not resist any such counsel or message from God to you. David says in Psalm 119:161, "My heart stands in awe of thy word." God looks with a gracious respect to those that tremble at his word (Isa. 66:2). When any duty is enforced by it, or sin condemned, we should submit to it with reverence and thankfulness. It is not a matter of liberty whether you will receive or reject the commands of God. But what God requires you must be cheerfully submitted to. Where matters are plain and unquestionable, as in duties of love to God and men, if in such cases men don't listen to the voice of God, he will surely require it of them.

To enforce this exhortation, I shall add the following considerations. 1. Neglecting to reform what you know to be amiss will determine you to be guilty of hypocrisy in your solemn transactions with God. Humiliation without reformation is not acceptable to God (Isa. 58:5-7). If one's heart desires to be reconciled to God, that individual would be willing to remove whatever hinders that reconciliation. If men believe sin to be as bad as they profess it to be, certainly they will be willing to let it go. But to pretend to desire peace and atonement with God while neglecting the terms on which he offers it, is to act hypocritically. To cry for favor and pardoning mercy while perpetuating the grounds of God's displeasure by continuing in sin is to mock God – to flatter him with your lips while your hearts are far from Him. It shows the carnality and selfishness of men's hearts in such prayers. As the Lord says in Hosea 7:14, "They assemble themselves for corn and wine, and they rebel against me."

2. Consider what sinners you have been, and still are, by not reforming the evils God has witnessed against you. It is a known fact that the sins of God's professing people are the provoking causes of their calamities. Micah 1:5, "For the transgression of Jacob is all this, and for the sin of the house of Israel." What did idolatry, oppression, and neglect of God's worship do but bring upon his people an abundance of misery? It is the abounding of iniquities among us that has made way for the many rebukes of heaven that we have been under. And neglecting to reform has continued them. Our own experience may convince us that we have forsaken God to our loss. As a result, we have lost his gracious spiritual presence in his ordinances and his protecting presence in his providences. What losses in your outward comforts, in your liberties, estates, and families have you experienced? Can we expect that God will change the methods of his providences, if there is no change for the better in us? Jeremiah 7:5-7, "If ye thoroughly amend your ways, and your doing ... then I will cause you to dwell in this place," etc. God is unchangeably just and holy. If we change our behavior, then we become subjects for his mercy to be expressed to. Surely the bitter fruits of sin should make every one willing to forsake it. Surely it is time to grow wiser, to say as Hosea 2:7, "I will go and return to my first husband, for then was it better with me then now." Some men try to advance themselves by sin, to get money and to raise their families by injustice, oppression, and a violent pursuit of the world. But

in doing so they bring shame upon their house. What are men likely to get by greediness, intemperance, and neglect of the great salvation provided for them through Christ other than sorrow here and eternal ruin hereafter?

3. If you reform what you know to be amiss, it will give ground to hope that God will show you what "you know not." God is ready to teach those that are willing to do their duty (John 7:17, Phil. 3:15-16). Job prays with confidence (Job 34:32), that God would "teach him what he knows not."

4. This will give hope that God will show a gracious respect to our prayers this very day. For God does not begrudge mercies to his people, if they are obedient. Isaiah 1:19, "If ye be willing and obedient, ye shall eat the good of the land." Would you not be willing to part with your sins that you may obtain these mercies? How reasonable are God's demands! He calls men to deny ungodliness and worldly lusts, to live soberly, righteously, and Godly in this present world. He calls us to love God and one another; and especially, to love your own souls, by being thoroughly careful to redeem the time. He tells us to turn to him in the spirit of a thorough repentance and to acknowledge our offences. God requires no compensation for the wrongs we have done him; no requitals for his injured name and glory, which has suffered so much by us. But if you will return to him with all your hearts, receive his redeeming grace, and resign yourselves to his prescribed service in sincerity, he will be gracious and present you with blessings of goodness. Zechariah 1:3, "Turn ye unto me, saith the Lord of hosts, and

I will turn unto you, saith the Lord of hosts." And can any be unwilling to this? Many are ready to say, "They would be willing to part with all kinds of money and to venture their lives that they might enjoy peaceable days again without distress. And will you not part with your lusts for it? Rid yourselves of unlawful liberties, be humble and holy that you may obtain it! "...and to him that orders his conversation aright will I show the salvation of God," (Psa. 50:23). Do you see, then, the danger of not reforming known evils and the inexcusableness of a knowing people refusing to be reformed? It is highly offensive to God, and shows men to be very faulty, when they will not reform what they know to be amiss.

The Great Salvation Revealed and Offered in the Gospel Explained

and a Hearty Acceptance of it Urged[3]

Outline of the Sermons

I. TEXT: Hebrews 2:3.

II. DOCTRINE: The salvation revealed and offered in the gospel is great and glorious, and the neglect of it will bring upon men great and unavoidable misery.

III. PROPOSITION I: That men need salvation, even such as the gospel reveals, made clear by considering,
   1. What man's natural estate at present is, how depraved and sinful.

---

[3] In Several Sermons on Hebrews 2:3. By William Williams, AM and Pastor of the Church in Hatfield. Luke 19:42, "If thou had known, even thou, at least in this thy day, the things which belong unto thy peace!" 1 Peter 4:17, "What shall the end of them be, that obey not the gospel of God?" Romans 11:20-21, "Because of unbelief they were broken off, and thou stand by faith. Be not high-minded but fear. For if God spared not the natural branches, take heed lest he also spare not thee." (Boston, MA: Printed by T. Crump, 1717.

2. What it is like to experience it here and hereafter; evils, temporal, spiritual and eternal.
3. Man's impotency to relieve himself under his present misery or prevent what is future.

IV. APPLICATION
1. USE 1: To reprove the carelessness of such who live as if they had no need of salvation
2. USE 2: To persuade men to endeavor to get a right understanding and thorough conviction of their need of salvation.

V. PROPOSITION II: There is a way of salvation revealed and proposed to men, in and by the gospel.
1. It reveals the eternal purpose and counsel of God concerning man's salvation.
2. It reveals that God has provided a Savior for perishing sinners, showing us who he is – God and man in one wonderful person.
3. The gospel makes an offer of salvation to all that enjoy it.
4. It propounds the terms upon which it may be had – faith, repentance, and a life of sincere obedience.
5. It is the great instrument and means God uses for the application of salvation.

VI. APPLICATION
1. USE 1: How exceedingly thankful we ought to be for the gospel.
2. USE 2: Let this cause you to consider, how are you the better for it?

VII. PROPOSITION III: That the salvation revealed and offered in the gospel is very great and glorious.

VIII. APPLICATION
1. USE 1: How greatly should men be concerned for the salvation of their souls.
2. USE 2: The reasons we must admire the riches of divine wisdom and grace herein.
3. USE 3: Exhortation, to secure an interest in this great salvation.

IX. PROPOSITION IV: Regardless of how great and glorious this salvation is, it is neglected by too many.
1. USE 1: The need for humiliation and mourning, that this salvation is so much neglected and undervalued.
2. USE 2: The need for examination to see whether you are guilty of neglecting this great salvation.
3. USE 3: To advise all that have neglected salvation to now embrace it.

X. PROPOSITION V: The neglect of this great salvation will expose men to great and unavoidable misery.
1. USE 1: The fearful blindness of many sinners who enjoy the gospel but neglect salvation.
2. USE 2: To awaken and reprove such as neglect the great salvation.
3. USE 3: Warning to all who have hitherto neglected salvation, not to continue in such neglect any longer.
4. USE 4: Exhortation to all who have professed and embraced this great salvation offered in the gospel, to live accordingly, to walk worthy of their privilege and profession.

To The Reader

Having been favored with reading the ensuing treatise, I desire heartily to bless God, who has graciously directed and led his servant here, assisted him in composing it, and inclined him to publish it. The subject is certainly the best that can be chosen for universal and perpetual use to souls, both for the convincing and converting of sinners and the quickening of saints. The design of this preface is, if it may please God, to impress the reader's soul with a serious consideration of the importance of the great and necessary truths here prepared for him, and to give very serious attention to them while he reads them. For how awakening should it be to hear of that great and glorious salvation revealed and offered to sinners in and by the gospel, and the great and unavoidable misery which the neglect of it will bring upon us. This great subject is here handled in the most plain and serious manner, with a pure aim and sincere zeal to inform the minds and enter the consciences of men.

Sinners are here shown how they stand in need of salvation. The way of salvation is opened; the great and glorious nature of the offered salvation is considered. Here also is shown how prone man is to neglect salvation, and the great and unavoidable misery which this neglect will bring upon men is faithfully and solemnly declared. These great things are here discoursed in a scriptural and rational manner; and the whole argument is managed in a method and style very solid and judicious, clear and distinct, earnest and moving, such as the weight, gravity, and solemnity of the subject calls for.

These are the doctrines which ministers should be intently fixed on if they would take heed to fulfill the ministry which they have received of the Lord. And these things must perpetually employ the minds of serious Christians in the working out of their own salvation, as well as be continually taught to sinners for their awakening and conversion.

But the great thing now to be desired and endeavored is that the reader may bring a mind seriously disposed to receive the truth, and that men would thoroughly consider these three things: this great salvation which was purchased by the Lord Jesus Christ for them and freely offered to them, the shameful neglect of it by Christians, and the damnation men bring upon themselves by neglecting it.

No wit or words of man can fully represent, and no tongue of men or angels can say, how *great* this salvation is. It is incomprehensibly great in its blessed and glorious author, the great God and our savior Jesus Christ. It is transcendently great in the price that purchased it, the blood of the Son of God. Inestimably great is this salvation for the many millions of immortal souls redeemed from the earth. And inconceivably great are its benefits to us: great are the evils, mischiefs, and miseries our souls are saved from and unspeakable are the positive mercies and blessings we are redeemed to – a salvation with eternal glory.

But how sad is it to consider how men despise their own souls by neglecting this great salvation! There are far too many Christians who have mere infatuation (and stupidity) who lightly esteem this rock of their salvation! How they disregard Christ, their souls, and heaven! And they disregard hell and damnation! With an equal profanity they disregard the wrath and curse of the eternal God as well as his favor, love, and blessing. This neglect of our selves is a most criminal contempt of God, and the one is not more disrespectful and ungrateful than the other is unnatural, unjust, cruel and barbarous. And what a dominion of sin and lust, what possession of Satan, what disbelief of the glorious gospel, and what aversion to true godliness do they infer?

We must ask ourselves, "how shall we escape if our salvation is too insignificant an interest for our concern?" Are the matters of our eternal welfare *trivial*?

That sinners would regard those fears which the word of the living God excites in them! That they would only sit down and solemnly ask themselves,

> "How can I expect to escape the vengeance of God? What will become of me in the end? Is not God's word true? Is not his wrath against unrepentant sinners unbearable? Can I be content to be the object of it? What can be more terrible than the words of his curse? Why should I bless myself and say, I shall have peace? Can my heart endure in the day when he shall deal with me? How can I read or hear the threatenings of God's law and not be utterly fearful?

Why should they not be to me in God's word, and in the mouth of his ministers, as if I heard them from the burning mountain, uttered in thunders or from the dark cloud bursting with flashes of fire? Can I be willing to be damned? Am I come to that point of ease in this understanding? Is my soul iron or marble such that nothing can make an impression on it? Do I not fear God being under condemnation, and indeed justly? Have I considered what damnation is? Is there anything so fearful that any other of our fears are equal to it? Why then do I not do everything I can to flee from the wrath of the almighty? Why do I run toward the point of his sword? Why do I dare test his vengeance? Why do I not listen now to my own conscience before it changes from a faithful monitor into my eternal furious enemy, avenger, and tormentor? Are its remorses and reproaches too hard to bear? The lashes and stings of it will be infinitely more torturing and piercing in the place of devils and of despair when the offer of salvation is never, ever to be made to me again, and the misery of excision from God becomes my reality!"

Sinners under the gospel should be reflecting, cherishing those wise and proper fears which are necessary to their effectual conversion to salvation.

But the treatise itself will supply the reader with more labored thoughts to this end. That which remains now for me to add is some apology for myself, that I allowed myself to be prevailed upon by a dear friend, my reverend brother, to put my name before his honored parents' book, who is also to me a father in grace and learning, and almost in years. This service to the public was intended by the late reverend Mr. Pemberton, of whose just esteem and high praise for the reverend author I have been long a witness.

The intelligent reader will easily perceive how great a master the author is in practical preaching, how well studied and experienced he is in the great doctrines of our holy religion, and with what art and labor he adapts his studies to the glory of God and the good of souls. God the Father of light, from whom every good and perfect gift comes down, has truly given him understanding to please and profit, convince, persuade, and direct. It is in the calm and still voice that the Spirit of God comes near to the soul, but oh with what light and power. In short, I esteem this a book worthy of the attentive reading of younger ministers, and to be well digested by those who may profit themselves not a little by it for the pulpit. Such preaching is the true glory and serves most under the blessing of God to prepare souls for heaven.

I pray God that the reverend author may live long to see the good effect of these and all his labors, both in the just and high esteem of his people and in their profiting under his ministry. And may he also see his learned sons shining after him in an excelling sanctity and usefulness.

Benjamin Colman
Boston, September 5, 1717.

Part 1

Hebrews 2:3, "How shall we escape if we neglect so great salvation."

The more light and grace God manifests to men in his transactions with them about their spiritual and eternal welfare, the greater obligation they are under to get a right understanding of their duty and to yield a ready and willing obedience to it. Their neglect of such a salvation will most certainly make their ignorance and sinfulness more voluntary and inexcusable and their punishment more intolerable. As the apostle shows in the first and second chapters of Romans, the giving of the law to Moses, and by him to the people of Israel in the wilderness, was a privilege attended with singular advantages. Therefore, the contempt and violation of it exposed the Israelites to greater and more severe penalties (Rom. 2:9).

And since this, the revelation of the gracious purposes of God in the gospel for reconciling and saving of both Jews and Gentiles by Jesus Christ, challenges the greatest regard from all those that are privileged with it, and the neglect thereof will bring on a proportionately greater punishment.

Our blessed apostle Paul showed an unparalleled zeal for the salvation of his countrymen, as we read in Romans 9. It is most probably concluded that he wrote this epistle to them (in some Greek copies this is expressed) specifically to persuade them to, and confirm them in, the truth of the Lord Jesus Christ as being the promised Savior of the world, in whom all the types and sacrifices of the law had received their accomplishment. However, he had been rejected and slighted by that unbelieving generation. So, to this end Paul instructs them in the transcendent excellency of his person, both with respect to his deity and humanity, as well as of his offices – that as a prophet he exceeded Moses, as a priest he exceeded Aaron, as king and priest he exceeded Melchizedek.

Having in the first verse exhorted them to an earnest application and intention of mind to the doctrine of the gospel delivered to them, he enforces it by several arguments in the three following verses. (1.) By a comparison taken from the punishment assigned to disobedience to the law, he argues a proportionate punishment shall be inflicted upon those who neglect the salvation of the gospel. Verse 2, "If the word spoken by angels was steadfast, and every transgression received a just recompence of reward, how shall we escape!" In giving the law, God made use of the ministry of angels. But he employed a more glorious person, even his own Son, in publishing his grace in the gospel. For this reason, the slighting of this gift is much more egregious than the contempt of the law. God justly expects that they who had slighted his servants would yet reverence his Son and receive his message, along with respect of the grace and love promised in it beyond what any enjoyed before. Therefore, its neglect would be more sinful than disobedience to the law, and the punishment would be more severe. Though he does not specifically declare here what the punishment shall be, we may gather it from other scriptures. One such example is Mark 16:16, "He that believes not shall be damned," as well as John 3:36 and 2 Thessalonians 1:8,9. But the manner of expression that the apostle uses shows it to be very great. How shall we escape? It implies there will be no way or means of escape, but rather unavoidable and inexpressible evil and misery will come to those that neglect (*i.e.*, slight, disregard, undervalue) or refuse this great salvation. Paul is referring to the gospel here as evident from the preceding verse. And the gospel is called *salvation*, for it represents the grace of God that brings salvation (Titus 2:11). And he calls it "so great salvation," to further amplify the grace of God in the revealing of it and to show the sin of neglecting it.

He further enforces this (2.) By the people that delivered this doctrine to them – first the Lord Jesus Christ himself, and next to him the apostles, who were his constant hearers and attendants. (3.) By the divine testimony that was given to this doctrine, by the presence and power of the Holy Spirit accompanying the first preachers of it with signs, wonders, various miracles, and extraordinary gifts (verse 4).

I shall not further insist on these things, but proceed to the doctrine, which by divine help I will now speak to.

DOCTRINE. The salvation revealed and offered to sinners in and by the gospel is great and glorious, and the neglect of it will bring upon men great and unavoidable misery.

I will speak to this doctrine under the following propositions.

1) That men need the salvation that God offers them.
2) There is a way of salvation, revealed and proposed to them in and by the gospel.
3) That this salvation is great and glorious.
4) That notwithstanding the greatness of it, men are prone to neglect it, and many do so.
5) That in neglecting this salvation, men will bring upon themselves great and unavoidable misery, such as they will not know how to bear and shall not be able to escape.

Proposition 1: That men need the salvation the gospel reveals. This is a truth necessarily implied in the text, and the very offer of it supposes man's necessity of it. It would be a reflection upon the wisdom, care, and mercy of God in contriving a way of salvation and revealing it to us, and urging it by so many arguments upon us, if we had no need of it.

But it may be evidenced that the state of all men is such that they have a great and absolute need of salvation, and a real sense and conviction of this truth will be greatly serviceable to awaken and excite men to a due concern that they may be interested in the salvation offered to them. Just as those who are sick value a physician, the truth of this proposition must be considered thoroughly because of the dismal effects of not doing so. Experience shows man to be a creature full of, and subject to, an abundance of misery.

And the scriptures give an account of the cause of it. As Romans 5:12 states, "By one man sin entered into the world, and death by sin, and so death passed upon all men, for that all have sinned." The first Adam conveyed sin and death to all his wretched progeny. All the children of Adam are all, together with him, sinful and miserable by nature, and consequently stand in absolute need of salvation. The truth of this proposition may be cleared up by considering,

1. What man's natural estate at present is, 2. What consequences he faces as a result and, 3. How unable he is to relieve himself from his present misery or prevent what is future.

1. Man's present natural estate shows his absolute need of salvation.

(1.) Every man is naturally destitute of the virtuous image of God, even of the knowledge of God, righteousness, and true holiness which was the image of God upon him when he was at first created. This was man's peculiar dignity at first, which nothing else in this lower world was capable of. This was a far greater honor to man than his empire and dominion over the world, because this rendered him capable of glorifying God and conversing with him. This is the highest honor that can be given to a creature. But this man fell from this originally created state, and all men have lost this goodness together with him. As Paul states in Romans 3:23, "All have sinned and come short of the glory of God." As such, no man naturally has a heart to know, to choose, or to love God as his chief good, to serve and glorify him as his last end, to seek after conformity to him and communion with him as his true blessedness. Rather, man has a natural disposition quite contrary to all that.

Now such a loss as this is an inconceivable misery, for because of the fall the original righteousness, harmony, and beauty of the soul is lost. Man is not like what he was when he came out of the hands of God. Surely man needs to have such a loss repaired, and by this his spiritual health and beauty restored.

(2.) The nature of man is universally corrupted. Original purity and morality being lost, there naturally follows a universal defilement and deformity of the whole soul, and it is wholly disordered and out of course in all those ways wherein it exerts itself. Where God's image is lost, Satan's image is introduced. Instead of a holy nature, there is a sinful nature. Instead of purity, there is pollution. God himself gives that testimony concerning man in Genesis 6:5, "That the imagination of the thoughts of his heart were only evil continually." Sinful motions do as naturally rise out of the heart as sparks from the fire, or filthy steams from a dunghill. And we find many holy men in Scripture acknowledging and lamenting this natural pollution, confessing its close connection to them from birth. David says in Psalm 51:5, "Behold I was shapen in iniquity, and in sin did my mother conceive me." Also, the apostle Paul in Romans 7:18, "I know that in me (that is in my flesh) dwells no good thing." Nature in and of itself is devoid of holiness and therefore cannot produce any holy actions. Job is also seen bewailing the corruption of nature in that expression in Job 14:4, "Who can bring a clean thing out of an unclean?" intimating that all are by nature stained and defiled. And as this pollution extends to all men, so its contagion overspreads the whole of man. Man is wholly corrupt; both soul and body are tainted with sin. Isaiah 1:6, "From the crown of the head to the sole of the foot, there is no part clean." Here the soul is naturally running to evil, readily embracing the solicitations it meets with as the members of the body are ready instruments of unrighteousness.

This may be illustrated in the several faculties of the soul.

1. The understanding, which is the leading faculty of the soul, is wholly corrupted. It is therefore full of mistakes and darkness in its understanding, erroneous in its judgment, foolish in its reasonings, evil in its designs, vain in its thoughts. Here low and unworthy thoughts of God proceed from it. Psalm 50:21 explains that when God offers himself as a fit portion and happiness for the soul, it can see no amiableness in him, but prefers "broken cisterns before the fountain of living waters." Without the powerful irradiation of the Spirit of God, the soul doesn't esteem the offers of God's mercy. It cannot see the evil of sin nor the good of obedience, but rather *calls evil good and good evil*. And if at any time the depraved soul recognizes virtue, it is rather from some respect it bears to himself than from its respect to the nature and will of God. What a treasure of folly and vanity is the mind of man! The one that truly sees and considers it will, with the apostle, see cause to cry out, "Oh wretched man that I am," (Rom. 7:24).

2. The will is also corrupt and reveals its nature in the various ways it behaves. Perverse in the choices it makes, preferring evil before good, controlled by a corrupt judgment or vicious appetite. Although there is a natural instinct after happiness, yet through the corruption of it, the will refuses true happiness when it is offered. It is tyrannical in its commands, without and against all sanctified reason. It is obstinate in evil and against good. As Jeremiah 1:25 declares, "We have loved strangers and after them we will go." This is the ground of Christ's complaint against the Jews in his time. In John 5:49 he says, "You will not come to me, that you may have life." And thus, God says of his people, their neck is as an *iron sinew* (Isa. 38:4) that would not listen to him (Ezekiel 20:8, cf. Exod. 32:9; Acts 7:51; Romans 2:5).

3. The memory which should be the treasury and storehouse of the soul of proper and seasonable truths for its direction and comfort, how unfaithful and unprofitable is it instead? How ready to receive and entertain and produce what is evil, and to exclude and let slip what is good? How often does God condemn and afflict his people for their forgetfulness of him and his favor? Psalm 106:21, "They forgot God their Savior." Psalm 106:7, "They remembered not the multitude of thy mercies, yea they soon forgot his works." And how much of the same are we guilty of? A forgetfulness of mercies and benefits, forgetfulness of vows and promises, forgetfulness of commands that are often urged and repeated. Our memories are like sieves that let out the flour and retain the bran. Through the corruption of this faculty the same sin becomes often repeated by us.

4. The affections of the soul are depraved and out of course. Here those things that should be loved, desired, and delighted in are disliked, rejected, and hated; and those things which should be hated are loved. God himself who is infinite, immutable, and everlasting good and should be loved with all the heart, soul, and strength is disregarded and slighted. And the perishing objects that the world offers are preferred above him. 2 Timothy 3:4 states, "That they are lovers of pleasure more than lovers of God." Jeremiah 2:13, "They have forsaken the fountain of living waters, and hewed out to themselves cisterns, broken cisterns that can hold no water." The creature is preferred above the Creator, and men are naturally seeking a false happiness in the profits, honors, and pleasures of the present life, while neglecting the love and grace of God. Yes, not only the perishing things of time are idolized, but carnal and sinful objects, forbidden pleasures that corrupt, defile, and debilitate the soul, are also eagerly pursued and inordinately delighted in.

5. The conscience is also woefully corrupted. Conscience is that power in man whereby he was made capable to consider, review, and pass a judgment upon his own actions. It is God's monitor in the soul, to accuse when we act contrary to the rule he has given us, and to approve when we do what is right. But because the mind is defiled, the conscience is defiled also (Titus 1:15). Sometimes through the prevalence of corrupt affections it loses its authority and does not discharge its office. Sometimes it is even said to be seared as with a hot iron. There is no remorse

for sin, no dread of future judgment, no care to have the guilt of sin removed, the heart purified, and justice atoned, as a preparation for it. Now the soul and all its faculties being in this way corrupted, it is in desperate need of salvation. So it *follows:*

(3.) Fallen man possesses a disposition to all kinds of actual sin. Such a darkened understanding, such a stubborn will, such a depraved state of soul is inclined to all kinds of evil. A corrupt nature exerts itself more in some ways in some people, and in other ways more in others. Yet there are no particular acts of sin that any fall into that the corrupt nature lacks a disposition to act the same. That spirit of pride and self-love that naturally governs every man will carry him to the same place if the temptation is offered. But though many are withheld from specific sins that others commit, yet there are none in their natural state that are not under the reigning power of sin and miserable tyranny of Satan. So, they commit numerous transgressions in thought, word, and deed every day. This is what caused the psalmist to say in Psalm 19:12, "Who can understand his errors?" and to lament in Psalm 40:12, "Innumerable evils compass me about, mine iniquities are gone over my head."

If our actual sins are investigated, they are like the hairs of our heads or like the sands on the seashore, numerous and beyond account. He that makes a thorough inquiry into his life and actions, does not know how or can't give account of one of a thousand. Where he takes notice of one, a thousand will escape his observation. What duty, what act of our lives can we find that is free from sin? If you should single out the best duty you ever performed, there might be many sins intermingled with it. Now, the wages due for our sin is death (Rom. 6:23). Every act of sin furthers the sinner's and binds the curse upon him. The righteous law of God condemns for every transgression; every sinful word, thought or action draws down vengeance on your head. So that every sinner stands liable to bear the curse of the law whenever the justice of God demands it of him. Were but men's eyes opened to see their sins, the truth of the threatening and the inflexible severity of justice, they would readily own that they are under an absolute necessity of salvation.

2. That men in their natural state need salvation will be further evident if we consider what misery awaits a sinful state and course of life. Sin is in itself the soul's greatest misery, and it has the greatest evils inherent in it. These might be enlarged upon, but I shall only hint at some under these three headings.

(1.) All temporal evils are the bitter fruits of sin. Death with all its associated diseases, pains, and needs which embitter life and hasten death are the offspring of sin. In Deuteronomy 28 (verse 16 to the end) Moses gives an account of the curses that sin would bring upon the people of Israel. A sinner is in danger of being cursed in his body, in his posterity, in his name, in his estate, and in all his designs and undertakings. While a sinner is oblivious to the curse of the law in an impenitent and unreconciled estate, he is in daily danger of one temporal misery or other which may either put an end to his life or embitter it to him. But what is worse than *this:*

(2.) Sin exposes men to be judicially left by God to spiritual evils of all sorts, of which Scripture and experience offers an abundance of sad instances. Some have been left to drunkenness, blindness of mind, and a hardened conscience, so that their foolish hearts are darkened with false conceptions about the plainest and most important truths. Then there are others who have been left to embrace errors. Others have been given up to wicked affections, whose hearts have been incurably hardened through the deceitfulness of sin. No sinner can tell how far a righteous God by way of punishment for sin may permit any of these spiritual plagues to come to him in this life. Therefore, to be delivered from the danger of them ought to be looked upon as a most desirable mercy. And yet beyond these,

(3.) Every sinner is in danger of eternal miseries in the life to come. Eternal death is a part of sin's wages (Rom. 6:23). Our Lord Jesus Christ who will be the glorious Judge of the world tells us what sentence shall be passed upon the wicked at the last day. As Matthew 25:41 says, "Depart from me ye cursed into everlasting fire prepared for the devil and his angels. The sentence is full of terror and may justly rouse the most sleepy and insensible sinners to tremble at it and engage them with greatest intention of soul to apply themselves to the blessed Jesus that saves from wrath to come. What comfort can he hope to ever enjoy that shall never enjoy God? What ease can he ever hope to find that will be surrounded with everlasting flames? How vainly does he bless himself whom Christ will curse? I *proceed:*

3. To show man's impotency to save himself from his present misery or prevent what is future. Man has destroyed himself, but it is beyond his power to save himself. Many have attempted it, and it is no easy thing to convince men of their insufficiency to do it. But it is a most certain truth that men cannot do this *for:*

(1.) He does not have power to recover his original state of holiness. Without holiness man cannot be happy, for the lack of holiness renders him unfit to enjoy God in which his happiness consists. That he cannot recover this is evident partly because the image of God was put upon man at first by a creating power, and wherever this is renewed it requires a like power. Nothing less than almighty grace is sufficient to transform the will of man to choose and love holiness. Psalm 10:3 states, "Thy people shall be willing in the day of thy power," and Eph. 2:10, "Ye are his workmanship created in Christ Jesus to good works." Partly because the depravation of the soul through sin is universal; all its faculties are corrupted. This means that the greatest arguments, the strongest persuasions, the greatest encouragements that are put before men will not incline them to it, until victorious grace effectually does it. As Philippians 2:13 states, "It is God that works in you both to will and to do of his own good pleasure," and 2 Corinthians 3:5, "Not that we are sufficient of ourselves to think anything as we ought, but our sufficiency is of God."

And partly because there is a natural, rooted enmity in the heart for holiness. So that man left to himself would never choose holiness for his happiness. As Romans 8:7 states, "The carnal mind is enmity against God, and is not subject to the law of God, neither indeed can be." There is a carnality of the mind as well as of the affections which diverts the soul from God and inclines him to love himself above God; and the more holy and spiritual any command is the greater resistance there is in the corrupt heart against it. The great controversy that men have against Christ is his government; they will not have him rule over them.

(2.) He can never recover the favor of God, nor by any act of his own regain the former peace and friendship that was between God and him or do anything that may entitle him to life. He cannot fulfil the duty required in the first covenant, which was perfect obedience to the law of God. As Ecclesiastes 7:20 says, "There is not a just man upon earth that does good and does not sin," and James 3:2, "In many things we all offend." The apostle Paul once had a great opinion of his own righteousness. But afterward when he knew himself better, when he understood the spiritual meaning and latitude of the law, all his confidence failed him, and he despaired even of life.

Neither can we bear the penalty necessary to satisfy the law and procure our release from the sentence of condemnation. The punishment for sin is death, even eternal death. Reason tells us that the punishment God threatens is suitable to the majesty of God against whom sin is committed. And God having established this, will proceed accordingly. It is therefore impossible that a sinner should procure his own discharge by bearing such a punishment. And indeed, if men could have paid the price due for their own sins, Christ's sufferings might have been spared.

I shall add a word or two of application, before I pass to the next proposition.

1. To reprove the false security and carelessness of those who live as if they had no need of salvation, though still under the guilt and power of their sins and oblivious to all the misery they expose them to. It might be expected that those who have the guilt of all the sins of their whole lives weighing upon them, every day liable to divine wrath and vengeance which they are neither able to bear nor escape, should give themselves no rest until they are delivered from this guilt and danger. But alas! How many are there with whom it is quite otherwise, who remain unconcerned and insensible. The guilt of sin is no burden to them; the wrath of God is no terror to them. And though offers of salvation are daily sounding in their ears, they are unaffected by them. To promote the awakening of such vile sinners, let me propose two or three things.

(1.) If you are not convinced of your need of salvation enough to seek after it, damnation will certainly be your portion. For there is no middle ground between these. Not only will you fall under the wrath and curse of God and be cut off from hopes of mercy and comfort hereafter if you neglect this, but yours will be a certain end; the ruin of impenitent and unbelieving sinners is positively declared. Mark 16:16 states, "He that believeth not shall be damned," and Romans 2:4, 9, while those who receive and obey Christ, and receive salvation by him, shall be admitted into mansions of joy and glory, of light and immortality: you must be cast out into outer darkness where there will be sorrow and shame, pain and grief, vexation and anguish. Were there any hopes of being hid from the revenging hand of God, this would be a plea to excuse your carelessness in this matter. But when it is certain that damnation and misery will be your portion and punishment if you continue in this estate, your carelessness is inexcusable. Is hell so easy a place, is the wrath of God so slight a matter, that you need not trouble yourself with any concern to escape it? Can you imagine bearing the revenges of despised mercy and incensed justice? Can you support the weight of the omnipotent one, the anguish of the never dying worm, the burning heat of those flames that never shall be extinguished? Surely the dread of damnation should make you concerned enough to obtain salvation!

(2.) There is nothing in the world that can make up for the lack of salvation or be a ground of comfort to you under the feeling of damnation. There are many things which sinners who are careless about their salvation divert themselves with and spend their time and thoughts about. Some are anxiously pursuing the profits of the world as if these could satisfy them. But suppose you could obtain all that profit, pleasure, and honor that you are reaching after and in the end fail to acquire salvation, will these comfort you? Surely our Savior ought to be believed when he tells us that man will not profit who gains the whole world and loses his own soul (Matt. 16:26). Though you may be respected and honored among men, can this satisfy you at the approaches of death, when you must appear before the judgment seat of Christ? On that day, all such things will appear to be trifles and vanities, wholly incapable of saving you from horrible torment in the flames of divine wrath.

(3.) Their present carelessness and false sense of security is a sad and very dangerous state arising out of the slumber of their conscience, the blindness of their mind, and the hardness of their heart. They are hardened through the deceitfulness of sin that listens to the flattering promises of profit and pleasure that it will yield them; and their love to it blinds them so they can't see the evil or danger of it but presume they will have peace, though they walk after the imagination of their evil hearts. They tell themselves that God neither minds their sins nor is offended by them. The apostle speaks of them in 2 Cor. 4:4, "Whose eyes the God of this world has blinded, lest the light of the glorious gospel of Christ should shine into them." And there is an abundance of methods he uses to this purpose, to promote false peace and an ungrounded hope in them.

2. Since man in his fallen estate needs salvation, let all be persuaded to apply themselves in order to get a right understanding and thorough conviction of their need of it. Though all need it, too many do not realize their need of it. Instead, they entertain presumptuous and self-flattering conceits of themselves. Like Laodicea in Revelation 3:17, They, "think they are rich and increased with goods and have need of nothing." They have no sense of their soul

dangers, so they don't trouble themselves to seek after a remedy. It's not only a duty charged by God but a point of wisdom for men to know their own state, to pass a right judgment upon themselves, and to know what the state of their soul is with reference to eternity.

Until you have a sense of your absolute need of salvation, you will not be thoroughly concerned to obtain it. It is that sense of the dire need, or an understanding of the worth of things, that kindles desires and excites endeavors in men to obtain them. Now such is man's natural aversion to God that he will not be concerned for his favor and pardoning mercy until he understands and feels his guilt and misery. It is the curse that drives men to the promise, and the dread of justice to the throne of grace. It is the sight and sense of sin that makes a savior with all his benefits become precious and necessary in the eyes of a sinner. The prodigal son never thinks of returning to his father until he believes himself to be perishing for lack of bread. In Luke 15:17 he says, "And when he came to himself, he said, 'how many hired servants of my father have bread enough and to spare, and I perish with hunger?'" And Christ tells us in Matthew 9:12-13, "Those who are whole do not need a physician, but those who are sick. I came not to call the righteous but sinners to repentance." And accordingly, the invitations of the gospel say as in Matthew 11:28, "Come unto me all ye that labor and are heavy laden, and I will give you rest." And Isaiah 55:1, "Ho every one that thirsts, come to the waters of life," and Hebrews 6:18, "Who have fled for refuge to lay hold of the hope set before them." According to the sense men have of their disease, so will be their cure and remedy. They that think they need nothing do not seek out a physician. None values bread but the hungry, none values water but the thirsty. Only those who see the avenger of blood at their heels make haste to the city of refuge. Insensible sinners do not see their need of a Savior; they who think they can atone for their own sins will not prize the blood of Christ. They who think they can subdue their own lusts and purify their own hearts will not apply themselves to the regenerating and sanctifying spirit to do it for them. We are all sinners, but God is merciful in that Christ died for sinners. It is for this reason especially that this proposition is so much insisted upon, that people may be awakened from their self-flattering dreams to serious consideration of their indispensable need of the salvation that the gospel reveals. To further a clear sense of need, let me offer the following advice.

    1. Do not evaluate and determine your state by false rules. Do not comfort yourselves with hopes of the goodness of your condition upon fallible and uncertain grounds. This is one thing that misleads many and lulls them into a false sense of security. If the rule is fallible, the judgment you pass upon yourselves will also be fallible. Now there are many false rules by which men are comforted. Some think their condition to be good because of they attend to the external duties of religion. This was the confidence of the pharisees in Luke 18:11, "I fast twice in the week, I give tithes of all that I possess." It is represented as a plea that some will make in the judgment day of Christ that will be rejected, Luke 13:26,

"We have eaten and drank in thy presence, and thou hast taught in our streets." External duties of religion with seeming devotion from custom, example, and education, as well as terrors of conscience, are worthless where there is no principle of grace in the heart. Others are comforted on account of their morality and conscientious behavior. They live soberly and righteously among men and do not indulge themselves in questionable practices. This was the confidence of the young man that came to Christ in Mark 10:20, "All these have I observed from my youth." Morality is amiable and commendable, but men may be moral either out of respect for their interest, or to promote their reputation and esteem among men, or they may even be scared into it through terrors of conscience and fears of hell. Conscientious men are not all holy. Still others comfort themselves because of the good affections that they often feel stirring; they feel sorrow for sin and mourn for their sinful behaviors. Their hearts are sometimes enlarged in the duties of worship they attend. They find some delight and joy in hearing the word. They are moved by the sufferings of Christ and the glory of heaven. They have desires after grace, *etc*. But one can have *religious* affections without *gracious* affections. There is a legal, as well as an evangelical, sorrow for sin. Judas was much bothered by his sin, and as you read, repented. Ahab humbled himself. The stony ground hearers received the word with joy and were much affected with it. Of John the Baptist's hearers you read in John 3:35 that they were willing for a season to rejoice in his light; they were awakened and moved by his ministry. The foolish virgins in

Matthew 25 desired oil with earnestness and concern. Balaam was affected with the blessedness of the righteous and desired it (Num. 23:10). From these many examples you can see that a moving of affection is no solid ground on which you may conclude your estate to be good. Finally, some attempt to comfort themselves because of some resemblances of grace that they have; they desire to be justified by the righteousness of Christ, they love some of the people of God; they have a heart open to help those that are poor and needy; they have a zeal against sin; they are willing to own and defend the cause of God and to improve their estates for the support of his worship and ordinances. But such things as these may be found where there is no true grace. A man may desire to be justified by Christ's righteousness, and yet not close with him upon the terms of the gospel. Men desire an abundance of things that they never attain. They may love some of the people of God for selfish motives because they have been beneficent towards them, not because they love God or his image appearing in them. And as for zeal against sin, it is many times partial or selfish. Jehu was zealous against the idolatry of Baal; but his zeal was wildfire and not born from holy anger against sin and love for the purity of God's worship. And men may be serviceable with their estates to the worship of God where there is no true grace. In 1 Chronicles 26:28 you read of things dedicated to the treasury of the house of God by Saul, Abner, and Joab as well as others.

  2. Be willing to put forth effort to come to the knowledge of your condition, that you may see your state as

it is. There are several helps which should be useful in doing so:

(1.) Search into and give weight to the testimony God gives in his word concerning it. The word of God is a glass that truly represents man's natural deformity and misery. It is the great discoverer of the hearts of men; it lays open the evil nature of sin and shows the sad issues of it. It is greatly profitable for conviction as well as for comfort. It would be to the sinner's advantage to search diligently into it and meditate upon it. By the law is the knowledge of sin (Rom. 3:20). By the word of God, you are acquainted with the truth that there is a universal corruption and defilement cleaving to your natures as in Genesis 6:5 and Psalm 51:5, "Behold I was shaped in iniquity, and in sin did my mother conceive me. And John 3:6, "That which is born of the flesh is flesh." Sin like a strong poison has diffused itself through all the blood and spirits of Adam's miserable progeny. It informs us that the noblest faculties of the soul are corrupted by it, "their mind and conscience is defiled," (Titus 1:15). And if the governing faculties of the soul are depraved, no wonder the affections and passions are tumultuous and disordered. God whose prerogative it is to know the heart gives us this account of it in Jeremiah 17:9, "it is deceitful above all things and desperately wicked." So that from such a heart nothing but sin is propagated into the life and actions such that even the plowing of the wicked is sin, and their praying is an abomination to God. And again, see the account the Scripture gives of your danger in Ephesians 2:3, "you are children of wrath by nature." It declares that the curse lies upon all that fail in the obedience the law requires. Psalm 7:11 says "that God is angry with the wicked every day." Now certainly you have reason to credit God's testimony, an exact knowledge of men and all things in his creation that is of such infinite perfection that he can be under no temptation to deceive us.

(2.) God has given you the ability to reflect on yourselves and your past actions, and surely conscience is not always so dull that it cannot be summoned to help bring sin to remembrance and to show you your transgressions. Has it been the business of your lives to get the knowledge of God and his nature? To have a heart disposed to love him, trust in him, and reverence him? Has it been your care to worship him according to his directions? To sanctify his name in your hearts, to sanctify his sabbaths, and account them holy of the Lord and honorable? Or has the contrary been obvious in an abundance of instances? When you look at your behavior towards men, have you fulfilled your duty in regard to the many roles and capacities you fulfill, or have there been numerous deficiencies and disorders in them? Have you wronged your neighbor in any way? Have you been envious of your neighbor's status or been discontented with your own? As the psalmist says in Psalm 40:12, "Innumerable evils have compassed me about, mine iniquities have taken hold upon me; they are more than the hair of my head. Therefore, my heart fails me!" And Psalm 38:4, "Mine iniquities are gone over my head, as a heavy burden they are too heavy for me!"

(3.) There is often a great deal of vanity and groundless confidence in the goodness of our hearts, even in those that acknowledge the errors of their lives. If men would just observe their own hearts and the many and various workings of sin in them, they would certainly acknowledge their need of sanctification and pardoning grace. Although the corruption of the heart may be sometimes restrained, it does not ordinarily lie so still and quiet that upon serious observation of its corruption it does not betray itself. There are several ways whereby we may come to a considerable insight into our own hearts, even though they are exceedingly deep and deceitful.

1. We may do so by tracing actual sins back to their proper source. Our savior teaches us that when he tells us in Matthew 15:19, "Out of the heart proceeds evil thoughts, murders, adulteries, thefts, fornication, false witness, blasphemies." And James 4:1, "From whence come wars and fighting among you? Do they not come from your own lusts?" Where do men's proud behaviors arise from if not from the pride of their hearts? From where do their evil pursuits of the world come but from the worldliness of their hearts? There is not a sinful word that ever came out of the mouth, or an evil action done in the life, without it was first conceived in the heart. How vile must the heart be!

2. Observe the present workings of your own hearts. Much of the evil of the heart might be seen if we would take better notice of them. Sin is continually at work in the heart, and we may observe it upon command. When duty is enforced, the heart is working to some degree against it,

murmuring at the strictness and holiness of the command as though God were a hard master. When sin is threatened or punished, men's hearts may grumble against it, saying the way of the Lord is not fair. Men may observe the corrupt workings of their hearts under the providences of God, whether merciful or afflictive. If God gives prosperity, how soon do men forget God and their neighbors? How soon do they fall into self-admiration as if their own righteousness had deserved it? And if God brings affliction upon a man, how soon does that man grow impatient with complaints and anger against God? They question why it should be this way with them when others are spared from similar difficulties. (See Psa. 73.) Without exercising faith in God, holy desires of soul after him and real brokenness of heart for the sins confessed to him, we are nothing more than self-seeking hypocrites. Our carnal desires govern the heart rather than give respect to the divine command to commune with God. As Paul says in Romans 7:18, "I know that in me (that is in my flesh) dwells no good thing!"

  3. Earnestly beg the Spirit of God to teach you. This is one great end for which the Holy Spirit is promised, that is, to convince the world of sin (John 16:8). None other than the Spirit can effectively apply the word to the heart, can thoroughly awaken the conscience, can lay open the secret workings of the heart and lead you into the labyrinths of deceit that lie lurking in it. None other than the Spirit of God can engage a man to diligently seek God, setting the sins of his life clearly before him and causing him to see them rightly. Without the Holy Spirit's guidance, our best efforts

to seek out our sin will come to little good. So, with great fervor of soul, go to God and ask for his Spirit's help to show you and teach you his ways. And you will see the operations of his Spirit working a blessed change in your heart toward him. Then as Ezekiel 36:37 says of God, "I will for this be inquired of by the house of Israel to do it for them." And once you are enlightened to see sin and its due punishments by the powerful teachings of the Holy Spirit, it will be impossible to neglect this salvation that the gospel reveals to you. Rather, you will immediately cry out to God for the application of it.

Part 2

Proposition II: There is a way of salvation revealed and proposed to men in and by the gospel.

Now the way of salvation into his revealed is designed to *change* and *answer to* the depraved condition of man. The gospel reveals a way for man's recovery and complete happiness. It shows how he may be delivered from the guilt and power of his sins, restored to God's image and favor, and prepared for the enjoyment of God and communion with him where his happiness consists. As in Titus 2:3, "The grace of God that brings salvation has appeared to all men." This doctrine of grace delivered by the gospel reveals a way of salvation to all men, that is, to all sorts of men. And on this account it is called "the common salvation." This doctrine of salvation was first preached by the Lord Jesus Christ himself, and afterwards by his apostles, as our text informs us. And the great benefit it brought mankind was one thing that encouraged the apostle to preach the gospel, notwithstanding the difficulty he met with. As Romans 1:16 says, "I am not ashamed of the gospel of Christ, for it is the power of God to salvation to everyone that believes." This gospel is a powerful instrument which God uses to bring life and immortality to light (2 Tim. 1:10).

Question: How does the gospel reveal the way of salvation?

1. It reveals the gracious and eternal purpose and counsel of God concerning man's salvation. That man so

deeply sinful, so justly miserable may be saved, natural light could not reveal how this could be. Though much of the glory of God is displayed in his creation, the wisest of men in the heathen world were at a loss to figure out where man's happiness and fulfillment exists. As 1 Corinthians 1:21 says, "the world by wisdom knew not God." The way of man's reconciliation to God was hidden from them. It is said to be a mystery hidden in God (Eph. 3:9), in his own breast, in the secret purpose of his own will; and to be kept secret since the world began (Rom. 16:25). It was gradually revealed first to Adam in that promise of the seed of the woman (Gen. 3:15). It was further revealed to Abraham and succeeding prophets. But the clear and full revelation of God's gracious purpose in the matter was reserved for the days of the gospel. Thus, it is said in John 1:17, "Grace and truth came by Jesus Christ." He who came from the bosom of the Father was able to lay open the purposes of his heart concerning man's restoration by the gospel; this matter is revealed in such a measure as the wisdom of God saw fit.

2. The gospel reveals that God provided a Savior for perishing sinners; and shows us who and what he is. One great design of the gospel is to describe the person and show the glory of the Lord Jesus Christ. As John 3:16 states, "God so loved the world that he gave his only begotten Son, that whoever believes in him should not perish, but have everlasting life." It informs us that Jesus of Nazareth, the Son of God, is the person designed for this work, that it was he who Moses and the prophets wrote about (John 1:45). It is he whose birth was celebrated by a multitude of bright and

heavenly spirits testifying to the shepherds. Luke 2:10 says, "Unto you is born this day in the city of David a savior which is Christ the Lord." It is he who was given the name Jesus because he should save his people from their sins (Matt. 1:21). He came to take the load of sin from wounded and burdened consciences. God the Father testified concerning him in many ways that he is the person appointed by him for this work and accepted of him especially by his exaltation. "God exalted him to his own right hand to be prince and savior," (Acts 5:31). It is the privilege of those to whom the gospel is afforded that they are assured of one God and one Mediator between God and men, the man Christ Jesus (1 Tim. 2:5).

And again, the gospel shows us what manner of person this Savior is. He is one whose name is *wonderful*. He is eminently so in his person, having the natures of God and man mysteriously united in one being. Through him the glorious condescension, wisdom, and grace of God eminently shines forth. We needed one sufficient to transact with an offended God as well as to relate to and be a surety for man. The Scripture takes care to particularly inform us of the reality of both natures in the person of Christ. The gospel declares him to be truly man in that it gives us the history of his birth, his childhood and manhood, as is common for all men. Luke 2:52 tells us that he grew in wisdom and stature. He did the behaviors and had the properties of a real body: he ate, he drank, he slept, he walked, and he discoursed. He not only had the appearance of a body, but the nature of a true and real body as well, one that was especially prepared for him. This is undeniably evidenced by his sufferings. His sufferings were real. He expressed groans and tears of a human body. His death was real; he became obedient to death, even the death of the cross. It is clear therefore, that he took our nature that he might be a redeemer for us, and not for angels (Heb. 2:16).

The Scripture shows that he was truly God, "the express image of his person," (Heb. 1:3) and "we beheld his glory as the glory of the only begotten son," (John 1:14) and "I and my Father are one," (John 10:30). His Godhead was evidenced by the many miraculous operations that he brought about. The miracles which Christ wrought were done by his own power and not as those which were done by Moses, Elijah, Elisha, and others via an extraordinary presence of God with them. This is why he ascribes them to himself in John 14:12, "the works that I do." The apostles were careful to disclaim their own power and sufficiency in the miracles that they wrought; they rather ascribed them to the power of Christ working through them. He that had power to work miracles himself, as well as enable others to work them, is truly God.

The necessity of his being such a wonderful person is made clear in the gospel, that he might be qualified for the offices he sustains – prophet, priest, and king... that he might reveal divine truths clearly, convincingly, and effectually to the hearts and consciences of men in such a way as men might be able to bear them... and that he might perform perfect obedience to the law for us, and to suffer the curse and penalty of the law for us that satisfaction might be given to offended justice in our name. As God he could not suffer, as man he could not satisfy God's wrath by suffering, but as the perfect God-man he could do both.

3. The gospel makes an offer of salvation to those that are chosen by God to be his children. Acts 13:26 states, "To you is the word of this salvation sent." The apostle does not say, "we have brought it you," but rather, "God has sent it." And 1 Timothy 1:15 says, "this is a faithful saying and worthy of all acceptance, that Christ Jesus came into the world to save sinners." God in the gospel not only declares that there is salvation to be had, that it is a thing attainable, but he invites those feeling their sense of misery *to receive the remedy that is offered*. In their soul sickness he urges them to apply themselves to a soul physician as it is their duty to do so.

4. The gospel propounds the terms upon which salvation may be had, or what man must do on his part to have the righteousness and merit of Christ graciously applied to him. As the salvation revealed in the gospel is a doctrine of grace, God does not force it on man but rather dispenses it in a way suitable to his own honor and the sinner's comfort. God does not expect any valuable compensation from the sinner for it, or any personal worthiness that would recommend the sinner's acceptance of Christ to him. Salvation is for the miserable; God's pardon is for the guilty. And yet there are duties to be done by those that expect to be the subjects of it. Now these *are*:

(1.) Faith in the Lord Jesus Christ. This is a grace expressed and described in the Scripture suitable to the state of a sinner. It is said to be a "coming to Christ." And John 6:37 tells us that "he that comes to me I will in no wise cast out." This implies the lost state of a soul wandering up and down for help and finding none, but upon Christ's call comes to him. It is expressed by receiving Christ. John 1:12 verifies, "As many as received him, to them gave he the power to become the sons of God." This implies the gracious offer that God makes to needy, famishing souls – Christ the Bread of God that gives life to the world. It is expressed by fleeing to Christ for refuge to lay hold of the hope set before us (Heb. 6:18). The wrath of a provoked God is a terrible thing to a sensible sinner, which none can defend the soul from. Christ Jesus is the only shelter. That faith which justifies a sinner is not merely an assent to a proposition, but an act of the will as well as of the understanding. A sinner, convinced of the truth of the gospel and of the sufficiency of Christ to answer the needs of his soul, who receives the offer that God makes and consents to take him as a complete savior, entirely depending on him for righteousness, grace, and life, that one is given faith by God (Eph. 2:8) and the effect of the Father's drawing (John 6:44).

(2.) Repentance is another duty which the gospel requires and which Christ as Savior bestows (Acts 5:31). True faith is accompanied with evangelical mourning and brokenness of heart for sin (Zech. 12:10). Repentance is required for our participation in the comforts of the gospel. It is a part of Christ's office to bind up the broken hearted (Isa. 61:1). Accordingly, repentance is a duty that has promises annexed to it. It was the command of Christ to his apostles when he sent them forth (Luke 24:47) that repentance and remission of sins should be preached in his name, and the apostles did so. As Acts 2:38 states, "repent and be baptized every one of you, for the remission of sins," and Acts 3:19, "Repent and be converted, that your sins may be blotted out." In vain do impenitent sinners promise themselves salvation by Christ. Men who love their sins and live in them are enemies toward God and must expect to be dealt with accordingly.

(3.) A life of sincere obedience is also required of those that would be the heirs of salvation. You read in Hebrews 5:9 that he became the author of eternal salvation to all that obey him. It was one end of Christ's sufferings, that he might purify to himself a peculiar people zealous of good works (Titus 2:13). And it is the property of true faith to purify the heart (Acts 15:9). The more it is exercised the more the work of sanctification is carried on. It not only shows the reasonableness of obedience for the honor of the redeemer, but it directs the soul to Christ as the fountain of all grace and spiritual life. It realizes the truth of the promises, encourages, and enables the soul to submit to Christ's government, to choose his laws, to follow the conduct of his word and spirit, to have a respect to all his commands, knowing that none but the pure in heart shall see God (Matt. 5:8).

5. The gospel is the great means or instrument God makes use of for the application of salvation to the souls of men. Here the apostle in Romans 1:6 calls it, "the power of God unto salvation." God exerts the power of his grace

through his word to move the hearts of men to a thankful reception of the salvation he offers them. The gospel does not merely report to us that salvation is attainable. Rather, it is a covenant offered in God's name, clothed with his authority, and accompanied with his presence, effectual to convey the privileges purchased by Christ and contained in it. Here Paul commits believers to God and the word of his grace, as that which builds them up and gives them an inheritance among those who are sanctified (Acts 20:32). And it is called in James 1:24, "the ingrafted word which can save our souls." This may more fully appear by looking at some special benefits ascribed to it.

1. It is the special means made use of by the Spirit in the work of regeneration. For this reason, as well as others, it is called the Word of Life. The conveying of spiritual life to a soul dead in sins and trespasses is the first thing that prepares a soul for an actual interest in the salvation purchased by Christ. Without a spirit of life there can be no acts of life in faith, repentance, or any other graces, and the spirit of life is wrought by the word. As 1 Peter 1:23 says, "We are born again, not of corruptible seed, but of incorruptible by the word of God," and James 1:18, "Of his own will he begat us by the word of truth." As God created all things at first by his almighty word – he spoke and it was done – so when any soul is created again in righteousness and true holiness, it is done by his almighty power accompanying his word. This power is not inherent in the word itself, but it is mighty through God whenever he pleases to give it efficacy.

(2.) It is the special means of begetting that faith by which men are united to Christ and made partakers of his righteousness. This is declared in Romans 10:17, "Faith comes by hearing, and hearing by the word of God." In order to believe, the revelation of a suitable object of faith is essential, an offer of salvation must be made, and this revelation and offer must be credibly attested to be from God. Now God does all this by the gospel: Christ is there revealed as the end of the law for righteousness to everyone that believes. There is an offer made and plentiful assurance given to the truth of its being from God. What Paul said to the convinced jailor is the voice of the gospel to every sinner, Acts 16:31, "Believe on the Lord Jesus Christ, and thou shalt be saved, and thy house." It is the promise of the gospel that is the warrant for faith.

(3.) The word is the great means of sanctification, of purging out sin and perfecting holiness in the heart. Christ prays for his disciples in John 17:17, "Sanctify them by thy truth, thy word is truth." Sanctification is a work that is carried on progressively until the new creature gradually arrives to perfection. As a means of advancing this we are directed in 1 Peter 2:2, "As newborn babes, desire the sincere milk of the word, that we may grow thereby." God in the gospel prescribes rules of holiness and tells us how we should walk and please God. He tells us how we should walk in every situation and condition. He teaches us "to deny ungodliness and worldly lusts, and to live soberly, righteously and godly in the world," (Titus 2:12). And in the gospel, he gives the most proper encouragements to holiness, and the weightiest and most pressing reasons to depart from sin. Now when these are believed and followed, they become greatly serviceable to promote holiness both in heart and life.

(4.) The gospel is the means of conveying comfort, joy, and peace to the souls of believers who stand in need of comfort from the various troubles, trials, and sufferings they are exposed to in the world. Now the way of comfort that God has provided is not by visions and voices from heaven, but by the word of promise in the gospel: "By this he gives strong consolation unto the heirs of salvation," (Heb. 6:17-18).

USE I. How exceeding thankful then should we be for the gospel, that it reveals a way of salvation for guilty man! It is indeed a thing so great that all the wisdom of the world could never have discovered. A perpetual night of darkness blanketed the face of the world, and the whole race of mankind was doomed to guilt and despair and under a fearful expectation of God's fiery indignation. But God scattered that darkness by breaking forth the light of the gospel. And we that are privileged to know it are under a special obligation to be thankful for it.

(1.) In that it is an act of special grace and mercy. God was under no obligation to man to do this for him. Men have no moral excellencies to commend them to God. Sin destroyed man of his native beauty, made him loathsome before God, who is of purer eyes than to behold iniquities. The justice of God was engaged against man. Further, God had no need of man's friendship and salvation. He could have contented himself to glorify his mercy through the holy angels and served justice upon fallen angels and men. Had God chosen to execute on Adam and his sinful progeny the threatening of the first covenant, there could have been no injustice or unreasonable severity imputed to him. The carnal minds of men are prone to object to the justice of God in the imputation of Adam's sin to them who had no actual being at that time and therefore never gave personal consent to the covenant transaction between God and him. But the equity of this might be evidenced from the unspotted purity of God, who is, "righteous in all his ways, and holy in all his works," (Psa. 147:17). God is subject to no error or partiality in any of his administrations. Further, common reason allows it to be both just and necessary in many cases for parents to act as representatives for their children and still count their children bound by their act. Besides, had all mankind been alive at that time and called to choose a fit person to represent them, no doubt they would with one consent have chosen Adam, especially considering how he was qualified for the trust placed in him.

(2.) Such grace is not the common lot of mankind. Though divine mercy has enlarged itself in these latter ages of the world beyond what it did in earlier times, yet there are many vast nations of the world who are still covered in gross darkness, in the region of the shadow of death. God who is the sovereign Lord of his own grace shows his liberty in this matter, and it is free mercy that is to be acknowledged in the manifestations of it to some while he denies it to others. Our Savior explains in Matthew 11:25-26,

"What did God see in you more than in them? You are not less defiled by nature than they are nor less exposed to justice; you are children of wrath by nature as well as they; you have no greater propensity to anything that is good than they do." Paul, speaking of himself and others before the grace of God appeared in conversion, says in Titus 3:3, "We ourselves were sometime foolish, disobedient, deceived, serving divers lusts and pleasures, living in malice and envy, hateful and hating one another." You are as unworthy as they, and they as capable as you of a share in this salvation had the sovereign pleasure of God so determined. So, to be the subjects of such distinguishing mercy calls for your praises to God!

(3.) In that it is a mercy we are in absolute need of. The more necessary any mercy is, the greater its value among men. Therefore, food and clothing, necessary for the preservation of life, are more important than extra amenities of life. And yet the eternal salvation of the soul is more necessary than these. We are undone without a Savior. Consider the desperate state of the heathen who perish through lack of vision; the desperate state of devils who never had a savior provided for them. Your eternal welfare depends on the gospel, an immeasurable misery will be upon you if you ignore it. A mercy so infinitely necessary is to be valued above all else. All other mercies may be better spared than the salvation of your souls. It would be better never to have seen the light of the sun than not to have enjoyed the light of the gospel that brings salvation.

(4.) It further calls for thankfulness that God's mercy continues long after it has been so much neglected and disregarded. How often have you received the grace of God in vain? Though you have such a need for salvation, you haven't had a heart to seek after it. Though it has been brought to your door and laid before you in the promises of the gospel, you haven't had a heart to receive it. Pray God doesn't say of you as he did of those in Proverbs 1:24, "I have called and ye have refused, I have stretched out my hands, and no man regarded." Or as Christ said in Matthew 23:37, "How often would I have gathered you? And ye would not." With what coldness and indifference, with what careless and unpersuadable hearts have you heard the most earnest call of grace in the gospel? And yet gospel salvation is still rejected by you. Is there not cause to wonder whether divine patience has grown weary of waiting on you? That God doesn't say of you as he did of them in Luke 14:24, "None of these men that were bidden shall taste of my supper." The wonderful patience of God in this matter can be ascribed to nothing but his undeserved mercy, and justly calls for your grateful acknowledgments. Oh, that the long-suffering of God might be salvation to you!

USE II. This salvation that is laid before you in the gospel should cause you to consider how you are better for it. God takes notice where he gives this privilege to men, what application they make of it. Note that parable of the fig tree in the vineyard (Luke 13:7). He observes whether the offers of grace he makes to men are received and valued or whether they are neglected and slighted. Our Savior called those that followed John the Baptist's ministry in Matthew 11:7, "What did you go out into the wilderness to see?" What aim did they achieve and what profit did they gain by his ministry? At that great day of accounting when the secret of men's hearts shall be judged according to the gospel, this same question will be asked of us. Therefore, it concerns everyone to look into his own life and determine what real saving benefit and advantage you have gotten by embracing the gospel. You have gained more knowledge than others, but have you gained purer hearts? Has the gospel been the power of God to salvation to you? This is what you need to consider with earnest. For if it has not benefitted you, it would have been better than you had never heard of the gospel. It is some excuse for those who live in places of ignorance that they continue in sin. But to live in sin in the clear light of the gospel removes all pleas and excuses (John 15:22). To have frequent calls to repentance, and yet be impenitent and hard-hearted! To be persuaded with offers of grace by Christ, and yet reject them and live in unbelief! To be called into fellowship with Christ in eternal glory, and yet at last to fall into eternal misery! How dismal and without excuse would this state be? Consider *here*:

1. That you are a sinner, you no doubt will acknowledge. But have your eyes been opened to see the numerous sins of your lives, and to see them in their horrid and heinous realities? Can you say with the sensible prodigal in Luke 15:21, "Father I have sinned against heaven and in thy sight"? Has your sin become an unbearable burden to you? Do you tremble under the terror of divine

wrath for your sins? Until sinners see themselves perishing, and all hope of saving themselves taken away, they will not in earnest seek a savior. They who think their sins are few or small, or believe they can atone for them themselves, will not seek a savior.

2. Have you gotten a spiritual knowledge of Christ's excellency and sufficiency through the gospel for those ends for which he offers you? Can you say with Paul in 2 Timothy 1:12, "I know whom I have believed, and I am persuaded he is able to keep that which I have committed to him against that day?" An awakened sinner has a deep sense of the value of his soul, and yet he is willing to trust Christ for the salvation of it. As such, he is made to see an excellency, suitability, and preciousness in Christ because God has given him a spirit of wisdom and revelation in the knowledge of Christ (Eph. 1:17). He is enlightened by the Spirit of God to see him as divine; a Savior able to save to the uttermost those who come to God by him (Heb. 7:27). This is a Savior whom the wisdom and love of God has provided, whom divine justice has accepted; one that has justly vindicated God's honor, bringing in everlasting righteousness and completely satisfying the penalty and curse of sin. One in whom divine fulness dwells. And when the gospel reveals that Christ to a man, he can willingly trust in him and consent to take him for his savior completely. At that moment Christ becomes precious to him (1 Peter 2:7). Such is his valuation of him that all other things fade away when compared to Christ. As Paul says in Phil. 3:8, "I count all things but loss, for the excellency of the knowledge of

Christ Jesus my Lord, for whom I have suffered the loss of all things and count them but dung that I might win Christ."

3. Has the gospel come with purpose to your hearts, to subdue your corruptions and lusts? This is the salvation Christ designed for his people, to destroy the works of the devil, the author and promotor of sin in the world. Now it falls to those who belong to God to make it their serious business and concern that, through the power of his grace, they will mortify that sin in themselves that Christ came to destroy. That infinite weight of divine wrath which lay upon the Lord Jesus Christ was the effect of vindictive justice for sin, and it is the most forcible argument in the world to induce those who receive the gospel to mortify sin in their life. If you hope to have an interest in the death of Christ, how can you live any longer in sin? How incongruous would that life be? Sin will be burdensome if the Savior is precious to you. Consider therefore, has the gospel had such an effect on you? Does it encourage you to deny ungodliness and worldly lusts? (Titus 2:12). Does it subdue the opposition that is in your hearts to the kingdom of Christ? Does it humble you for sin, excite repentance, engage to watchfulness against it?

4. Do the hopes of the gospel excite you to a life of holiness? Does the gospel message cause you to perform your duties to God willingly and cheerfully? The grace of God that brings salvation teaches us not only to deny ungodliness and worldly lusts, but to also live soberly, righteously, and godly in this present world (Titus 2:12). To live in this way is to answer the design of Christ (verse 14),

"who gave himself for us, that he might redeem us from all iniquity and purify to himself a peculiar people, zealous of good works." The gospel is not only the means of conveying the spirit, who is the glorious author of holiness, but it presents the strongest arguments to further holiness. It gives us not only the pattern and rules for living holy, but also the promises and rewards of doing so. Both our present benefits in Christ and future hopes from him should constrain and engage us to live holy before him. Do you see the excellency, wisdom, and goodness in his divine commands for us to live holy? Do you truly desire to meet Christ in the day of his glorious appearing as your bridegroom and not desire to be as a bride adorned for her husband? Do you hope shortly to be with the Lord, to see him as he is, to be made like him, and not love and labor to be like him now? Surely if the promises of the gospel are believed, they will excite you to purge yourselves from all filthiness of flesh and spirit, and to seek perfect holiness in the fear of God (2 Cor. 7:1).

  5. What support does the gospel offer you against the troubles of life or the fears of death? Those who have received the testimonies and promises of divine grace as their heritage forever make them their songs in the house of their pilgrimage. This is one way God's people can be witnesses to his covenant truth and faithfulness. Our blessed Lord foretold his disciples in John 16:33, "In the world you shall have trouble, but in him you shall have peace." Here on earth, we meet with afflictions of various sorts – sickness, pains, losses, reproaches, hatred, and

persecution from the world and temptations from Satan. Do you now allow the promises and consolations of God to bear you up and revive your spirits under these sorrows? Do you allow him to enable you to show patience, meekness, and a quiet submission to his divine will in these times? Can you sustain your strength through spiritual comforts when outward comforts fail? Encourage yourselves in the Lord your God as David did in 1 Samuel 30:6, "David was greatly distressed because the men were talking of stoning him… But David found strength in the Lord his God." Christians need the assistance of the Holy Spirit to support them with the promises in times of need and to comfort them against the fears of death. Can you not by faith see and hope for a better inheritance than any the world offers? It is the special privilege of believers that they are begotten to a lively hope of an inheritance incorruptible and undefiled, reserved in heaven for them (1 Peter 1:3-4). And this hope enables them not only with a calmness of spirit and submission, but sometimes also with joyfulness to resign their spirits into the hands of God when death comes to summons them.

Part 3

Proposition III. That the salvation revealed and offered in the gospel is very great and glorious:

Carrying in it the brightest displays of the divine glory and containing in it the greatest mercy. The apostle calls it a "great salvation." The manner of his expression is worth our observation, "so great salvation," an inexpressible, yes, inconceivable greatness! This salvation is beyond any other gift that God ever offered to men. God performed many great wonders from the beginning of the world, but the salvation of sinners by Jesus Christ is beyond all comparison. As John 3:16 describes, "God *so* loved the world that he gave his only begotten son." The love evidenced by this gift is inexpressible! We read concerning the works of God in general that they are great! Honorable and glorious (Psa. 111:2-3). The works of creation and providence are such that they fill the hearts of considerate beholders with wonder and astonishment that cannot be understood. This is eminently true of God's work of redemption, the salvation of sinners by Jesus Christ, for which the praises of God will be celebrated throughout the days of eternity. There are so many great and mysterious wonders contained in it, such inestimable blessings accompanying it as may justly render it marvelous in our eyes. The only way to fully declare the greatness of this salvation would be to possess an understanding capable of comprehending it.

1. Consider what great difficulties lay in the way of it, and what a glorious display of divine perfections there was in bringing it to pass. This work of saving sinners had sufficient difficulties in the way of it that quite exceeded the wisdom of men or angels to remove. It was beyond them to determine how the sinner could be saved and, at the same time, sin condemned. How can mercy be exercised without the rights of justice being impaired? How could the honor of God's truth in the threatening of death to sin be vindicated without the death of the sinner? How this could be done, and man be preserved from everlasting ruin was above comprehension. But the wisdom of God surmounted all these difficulties, such that there is no breach in the harmony of his divine attributes. The wisdom of God created a way wherein his truth, justice, and mercy might all be glorified. As the psalmist observes in Psalm 85:10, "Mercy and truth have met together, righteousness and peace have kissed each other." In this is a glorious display of the Godhead and its perfections. Much of the divine glory and particularly that sacred mystery of the trinity of persons in the Godhead is more revealed in this work than any other before or since: God the Father contriving, God the Son performing, God the Holy Spirit applying salvation to fallen man. This counsel of peace was among these sacred persons before time, but their particular and distinct operations in and about it are in time exhibited in the gospel to raise our admiration and praise! And in this the glorious perfections of the Godhead are displayed more than in any other works. The power, wisdom, and goodness of God which appeared

in creation in the variety of creatures that were made, and adapting them to their respective ends, appears in this work with yet a greater luster over and above. Here God's holiness, truth, justice, and mercy, shine forth in their transcendent excellencies. The glory of the divine perfections never so displayed itself as it does in this wonderful work of bringing about salvation for sinful man. So much so that you read in Scripture that the heavenly spirits, the angels, desire to stoop down and look into this wonderful work (1 Peter 1:12)!

2. It may appear so if we consider how great and glorious a person was employed to purchase salvation for us. This work was undertaken by the Son of God himself, and obtained through his incarnation, obedience, sufferings, resurrection, and intercession. We may justly infer the greatness of the work from the glorious dignity of the person employed to perform it. None other than the only Son of God's love, in whom he was well pleased, was found worthy or capable to manage such an affair. Now the Son of God being so highly esteemed, so dearly beloved, would never have been employed to perform a small matter. This manifestation of divine glory, however, required that so great a person should be entrusted with this work. You read in 1 Peter 1:18, "We are not redeemed with corruptible things as silver and gold." No such price was of value sufficient for the redemption of a soul, much less of all the souls of the elect. But the precious blood of Christ, of God incarnate, was essential to procure such an inestimable benefit; otherwise, the outcome would have been insufficient. There

was no hope of having life by the law that was weak through the flesh (Rom. 8:3). Man's sinfulness had rendered him subservient to death and incapable of the righteousness the law required of him, acceptable for his justification. Nor would any of the sacrifices or ceremonial purifications of the law be sufficient. It was not possible that the blood of bulls and goats should take away sin. All these ceremonial rites could not take away the guilt of sin because they were never designed by God in their institution and establishment to do so. It was a work too great for an angel to have performed, for infinite wrath would have been a burden too heavy for any mere creature to have endured. The greatness of this salvation in respect to the person employed for the purchase of it might be further illustrated by considering what he did in order to secure it.

(1.) He assumed a human nature alongside his divinity. This is a doctrine that the scriptures expressly and plainly insist on. They also declare why it was necessary he should do this – that he might be a fit person to sustain the office of a surety in our stead, as having a true human nature he could adequately satisfy man's sin debt to God (Heb. 2:16). The reason the fallen angels are not saved is because there is no surety provided in their nature to transact for them. But Christ Jesus assumed the nature of man that he might make satisfaction in that same nature that had sinned; and therefore, a body was prepared for him because other sacrifices were not sufficient (Heb. 10:5-10). What a glorious and wonderful thing! That the human nature should be thus exalted in the one who was the brightness of his Father's glory and the express image of his person, "who thought it not robbery to be equal with God, should be made in the likeness of men," (Phil. 2:6-7). That God was manifest in the flesh, the apostle calls "the great mystery of godliness," (1 Tim. 3:16). This astonishing condescension is that which saints and angels will admire throughout the ages of eternity.

(2.) In submitting to a life of obedience. It is said in Galatians 4:4, "He was made under the law." He who was the supreme Lord, who had given laws to angels and men was made man, subjecting himself to his own laws. He became obedient both to the moral law and to the law of a mediator. He came from heaven not to do his own will but the will of his Father, and this he delighted in and submitted himself to. So that in this he became obedient *unto death*, even the death of the cross (Phil. 2:8).

(3.) The greatness of this work. Sinful man owed a debt of punishment by law, and this must be discharged. The wisdom of God saw it necessary that the law should not be abrogated; its punishments must be endured that justice might be glorified. Therefore, the Lord Jesus Christ sustained the role of our mediator when he undertook to suffer, to die, to shed his blood, and to make his soul an offering for sin, that he might redeem his church with his own blood (Acts 20:28). He submitted most freely and willingly to a state of suffering, he endured that grievous agony in the garden, where his sweat became like great drops of blood. He subjected himself to the cruel and unjust scourging, condemnation, and ridicule of Pilate and the

Roman soldiers. He allowed himself to be crucified and laid in a grave. Our glorious Lord Jesus endured an accursed death that he might redeem us from the curse of the law. For the Scripture abundantly informs us that his death and sufferings were in the nature of a sacrifice explicitly carried out as payment for our sins, and not for his own; for he was of perfect purity and innocence. None could ever convince him of sin nor charge any manner of fault against him, though his enemies with great malice attempted it. Rather, he was made sin for us who knew no sin himself, that we might be made the righteousness of God in him (2 Cor. 5:21 and Isa. 43:4-6). Now this being necessary for our salvation shows it to be inexpressibly and inconceivably great! There is no higher demonstration of love among the dearest friends that have ever been in the world, than to give their lives for each other. "But Christ commended his love beyond this, that while we were enemies he died for us," (Rom. 5:8, 10). That so glorious a person as this Godman should groan and sigh under the burden of divine wrath and expose himself to such painful and reprehensible sufferings! Even to death itself! This was such a work as astonished creation! It caused both the earth, as well as the obstinate hearts of his persecutors, to tremble. Such a work has never been done from the beginning of the world, nor shall ever be again to the end of it.

(4.) Having performed the work of his humiliation, our Lord Jesus Christ, conqueror over death and hell, rose from the grave, ascended into heaven, is crowned with glory and honor, and lives continually to make intercession for his people. His resurrection was a glorious and eminent proof of his satisfaction of the law. The law threatened death to sin; so, in order for the sinner to live, the surety must die. But in order that the sufficiency and acceptability of his death unto the ends for which he suffered might appear, he must rise again and not be held under the power of death.

His resurrection plainly showed that God accepted the death of Christ as a sufficient ransom for our sins. The active and passive obedience of the Lord Jesus Christ was in every way enough to free us from sin and condemnation by sin. But his resurrection served as visible evidence of the satisfaction of his death. This is ascribed to the Father as his discharge of him as Hebrews 13:20 explains, "The God of peace which brought again from the dead our Lord Jesus Christ." And in this a special ground of comfort is afforded to believers, in expectation of the blessings of a pardoned estate. As 1 Corinthians 14:17 says, "If Christ be not risen then you are yet in your sins." And again, Romans 4:25, "He died for our offences, and rose again for our justification." This act of his is convincing proof that he is indeed the Son of God and savior of the world, and not an impostor or deceiver as the Jews wickedly indicated. His own life demonstrates that he is capable of conveying life to others, which if he had remained in a state of death he could not have done (John 14:19). And the value of the resurrection is further discovered in that he not only rose but ascended to the right hand of God. This is a pledge and proof of his complete victory over all his enemies and shows how fully his redemptive sacrifice was accepted by the Father. Such glorious dignity and honor put upon him carries strong ground of encouragement to his people to commit themselves and all their concerns into his hands (Eph. 1:20-21, 1 Pet. 3:22). He is gone into heaven where angels, authorities and powers are now all subject to him. A further privilege following hereupon is his intercession for his people. He is in all respects accomplished for this work, and a person so tenderly loved and so highly honored that he shall not be rejected in any of the requests that he makes for his people as 1 John 2:1 indicates, "If any man sin, we have an advocate with the Father, Jesus Christ the righteous." (Also Heb. 2.14-17). And it is upon these several acts of his death, resurrection, ascension, and intercession that the apostle lays the foundation of his own triumph, as well as that of all believers (Rom. 8:33-34). From the consideration of the things spoken here, there is ground to conclude that if the manifestation of the glory of God in the salvation of his elect had not been a thing of such weight and importance, such great things would never have been accomplished to bring it to pass.

3. The greatness of this salvation might also be argued from the necessary, gracious, and effectual operation of the Holy Spirit in applying it to the souls of men. Not only the coming of Christ, but also the coming of the Holy Spirit signal the favor God manifests to mankind. Both were necessary to bring salvation to the souls of men. The Lord Jesus Christ satisfied the justice of God and procured favor for sinful man. And the descent of the Spirit was a sure testimony of it. Further, the presence of the Holy Spirit

comforts his disciples when they are saddened with the thoughts of his absence from them (John 16:7). And though the church in all ages have been in some degree privileged with the presence of the Spirit, the more plentiful communications of the Spirit was reserved for the times of the gospel (Acts 2:38). Accordingly, the apostle calls the gospel "the ministration of the spirit," (2 Cor. 3:8). And on this account, he points out the folly of the Judaizing Galatians who had grown fond of the Mosaic rites, by reminding them of the privilege they had gained by the gospel (Gal. 3:2). In 1 Peter 1:12, the gospel is said to be "preached to you by the Holy Spirit sent down from heaven." To this end, there were several gracious operations of the Spirit: to convict of sin, to open the eyes of the spiritually blind, to awaken the consciences of sinners, to show them their guilty, polluted, perishing condition without a Savior, to lead them to the knowledge of the sufficiency of the remedy revealed in it, to regenerate the soul, disposing and inclining it to a new life, and to assist in the work of sanctification, of which the Holy Spirit is the principal author. Now that so gracious a person as the Holy Spirit should be employed in this work of salvation also shows the work to be great. But *further,*

    4. That it is a great salvation will appear if we consider from what evil and misery we are saved. The greater any evil is from which a person is delivered, the more significant his salvation from it. To be delivered from tormenting pain, from cruel bondage and slavery; from the apprehensions of present death, are great things indeed.

(1.) This is a salvation from sin. For this reason, Christ was called "Jesus," (Matt. 1:21), because he saves his people from their sins. Sin invaded the whole race of mankind. The whole nature of mankind (the man Christ Jesus excepted) was and is stained and corrupted with it. All are under sin. Now sin is of all evils the greatest; there is no good in it. It is a worse evil than any affliction that men have suffered or can suffer in this world. It is worse than death, yes than death in the most frightful aspect that it ever appeared. Here many of the wisest and best men have chosen to suffer all sorts of tortures and the cruelest death that their enemies could inflict rather than yield to sin. Sin is in utter opposition to God; it is in opposition to his will and glory. Sin is a rebellion against God, a fighting against him, an attempt to blemish his wisdom, knowledge, justice, truth, holiness, power, goodness, patience, and mercy. Therefore, sin makes the sinner loathsome and abominable in the eyes of a holy God.

Sin is an evil that debases, defiles, and destroys the soul (Prov. 8:36). Sin is a resemblance and imitation of the devil (John 8:34, 1 John 3:8). The more men sin, the more they strengthen the devil's kingdom and fall in with his design. This being the universal inclination of depraved nature to choose and serve sin, it must indeed be a great and glorious work of divine grace to save and recover man from it, to change this wretched disposition in him, to subdue a heart to God that was formerly so full of rebellion and opposition against him, to cleanse a soul so deeply defiled, to create a clean heart and renew a right spirit in him, to turn that man from darkness to light and from the power of Satan to God (Psa. 51:19; Acts 26:18), and to make such a soul holy, to prepare it to love, fear, and glorify God, and to live to him forever. This is further confirmed if we consider man's impotency to work such a change in his own soul, his reluctancy against it, and the various methods he uses to continue in it in order to frustrate the designs of divine grace to effect it in him.

(2.) It is a salvation from hell. Sin is the worst of moral evils, and hell is the worst of penal evils. But Christ also saves his people from this. As 1 Thessalonians 1:10 states, "Jesus who delivered us from the wrath to come." Offended justice prepared hell for the vindication of divine glory in the everlasting punishment of sinners, and there they must feel the full weight of divine wrath. Now the Lord Jesus Christ by satisfying the payment for sin and bearing the curse of the law saves his people from it; so that they shall not come into condemnation. The miseries of hell are inconceivable! Therefore, salvation from it is rightly considered to be a great salvation.

(3.) This is a salvation that encompasses the mitigation and sanctification of all temporal evils that the people of God are exposed to in this world. It is one great and gracious fruit of the love of God in Christ toward sinners that though in his fatherly wisdom he corrects them, yet their chastisements are medicinal, not penal and vindictive. Designed by love to their spiritual profit, they have many comfortable promises belonging to them. And these are all ordered in such seasons and in such a measure as divine wisdom and love see to be best. Further, through them all the grace of Christ supports and consoles them. This ought to be counted no small nor menial privilege.

5. That it is a great salvation which the gospel reveals and offers to sinners by Christ may further appear, if we consider what blessings are contained in it and what privileges it entitles believers to. In addition to the freedom from evil, there are many positive blessings belonging to this salvation that are invaluably great. The profit or comfort of any outward blessing raises our esteem of it, and the more available it is to our present or future good, the more it is sought after.

They who are called to partake in this salvation are brought into a state of peace and reconciliation with God. The dreadful breach that sin had made between God and the sinner is corrected (Rom. 5:1). Peace with men is desirable, peace of conscience is more desirable. But peace with God is most desirable of all!

Again, their sins are forgiven, and they are made righteous before God through the imputation of the righteousness of Christ *unto them* by faith (Rom. 8:12). That vast debt which they owed is cancelled. God received full satisfaction for it in the surety of Christ, and upon believing, he freely, fully and forever discharges them from it. Now this is a blessed privilege and makes those happy that obtain it (Psa. 32:1-2).

And on this their persons and services are accepted (Eph. 1:6). Their hearts are sanctified, and they are graciously renewed and restored to some conformity to the divine image and likeness (2 Pet. 1:4). They have the promises of preservation in a state of grace, that the good work begun in them shall not be so obstructed by remaining sinfulness but shall in due time be perfected in them. Those weak beginnings of grace through the powerful and abiding presence of the Spirit of grace shall be preserved and cherished until they arrive at the stature of perfect men in Christ. Such a promise was never given to Adam in his state of innocence.

They also have liberty of access to the throne of grace, and encouragement to expect that they shall obtain mercy and find grace to help in all times of need (Eph. 2:18, Heb. 4:16). How much comfort and solace does this bring to gracious souls? That they have such a wise, powerful, and gracious God to go to in all their wants, fears, and temptations? Here also they have gracious communion with God. There are special seasons wherein he makes them glad with his countenance, leads them into the understanding of his excellencies, shows them the stability of his covenant, shines upon their graces, and fills them with unspeakable consolation.

Further, they have the privilege of adoption, they are honored not only with the title of children but have the real privilege of such (John 1:12, 2 Cor. 6:18). They have a child-like spirit of love, reverence, and obedience toward God. They have his fatherly care of them while here; and they have a child's portion and inheritance, reserved for and promised to them in the hereafter (Rom. 8:17). And this is so rich and great, so full and complete as to exceed all their desires and expectations. On all these accounts the privileges of salvation are great. But were there no more than their full enjoyment of God in a state of heavenly glory, this would be enough to convince us that it is so. To be ever with the Lord, to behold his face in righteousness, is a great thing indeed!

USE I. How greatly concerned men ought to be for the salvation of their own souls, and with what weight this matter should lie upon their spirits. The soul in a principal manner is the subject of this great salvation we have been speaking of. It was the soul especially that was stained and corrupted with sin, that needed to be restored by sanctifying grace. It was the soul that was first subjected to the impressions of divine wrath, and that can have the deepest sense of it. It is the soul that can know love and fear. It is the soul that can glorify and enjoy God, and it was the tender compassions of our Lord Jesus Christ working towards our precious but perishing souls which (next to the glory of his Father) moved him to do what he did for the salvation of them. The wisdom of the Father, the love of the Son, and the grace of the Spirit was in this way employed to bring about salvation for our lost and dying souls! How abundantly may this convince us of their great value, and engage us to a deep concern for them, that it may be well with them. There is no design that men have to carry on, no business that they have to do, of equal weight with this; none which deserves such regard from them. Surely if we consider these things as we ought, it would be impossible that our souls should be neglected as they are.

(1.) God knows the worth of our souls. He that made them knows the value of them: he knows their nature, their capacity, what vast desires they are filled with, and what eternal happiness they are capable of. Shall we then have such low thoughts of them, as only to think them fit to continue for the body, to be enslaved to flesh and sense? It would be a sin and shame for us to be careless of and unconcerned for them.

(2.) Consider, how great a danger you are in of losing your souls and failing in the salvation of them. The soul, as precious as it is, may be lost. Too many in every generation of men find themselves to be lost. Therefore, there is a sentence of death and condemnation now upon you. This is true of you as soon as you become one of the children of Adam (Eph. 2:3). We are children of wrath by nature, and it continues as long as we abide in unbelief (John 3:18). None but Christ can deliver you from it by presenting himself to justice in your stead. And yet, because of your ignorance of Christ's excellency and your natural aversion and unwillingness because of pride, spiritual laziness, love of sin, the snares, and allurements of the world, to come to him for the salvation he has purchased. There is danger regarding the many subtle attempts that Satan the great adversary is using to destroy your souls. He goes about as a *roaring* lion seeking whom he may *devour* (1 Peter 5:6). He hunts for the precious life; these are the souls of men that he would prey upon. He has already drawn you into an abundance of sins, and is daily tempting you to more, that he might bring upon you a dreadful destruction. Should not the danger you are in awaken your concern for your sins?

(3.) Consider that the loss of your souls will be very dreadful. Men have deeply mourned other losses they have met with, but who can conceive how dreadful and bitter the complaints of those who lose their souls? The loss of the soul does not consist in the annihilation of it, but in its separation and banishment from God and its being sentenced to the eternal regions of darkness and despair. How sorrowful will it be to be excluded from the kingdom of heaven, when others shall be admitted to it! To be thrust down with infernal spirits and damned souls into the pit of hell! When others sit down with Abraham, Isaac, and Jacob in the kingdom of God (Matt. 8:12), how horrific will it be to be sentenced to eternal separation from him! To be excluded from any comfortable sight of God, when others shall be encircled in the arms of his love, enjoying a state of satisfying fellowship and communion with him. How horrible will it be, to be a monument of divine wrath, to feel the weight of revenging justice for all eternity when others shall taste and experience the love of God and drink of the river of his pleasures? These things are dreadful beyond what our narrow understanding can comprehend! And it will further enhance these miseries that there will be no temporal pleasures to divert their thoughts from the afflicting sense of them, as it was with the rich man in the parable in Luke 16:24, when he could not have even a drop of water to cool his scorched tongue. If there were any hope that there might ever be an end of them, this would be some mitigation of their misery. But the truth that in hell the worm never dies, and the fire is never quenched, fills the soul with the most tormenting despair!

USE II. How much reason we have to admire the riches of divine wisdom, grace, and love which has provided such a great and glorious salvation for us. We read in Psalm 111:4, "He hath made his wonderful works to be remembered." God would not be forgotten in the world; therefore, he has set before us evident marks of his perfections in his works of creation and providence which are to be reflected upon. But his divine perfections shine forth most illustriously in the work of redemption; and in this especially our thoughts should be employed that our souls might be filled with a suitable understanding of salvation. And for this great work God should ever be glorious in our eyes! The psalmist contemplating the works of God cries out with admiration and praise in Psalm 8:4, "What is man that thou art mindful of him, and the son of man that thou visit him!" So great is the distance between the great and holy God and sinful man that we have reason to look upon this wonderful condescension from the point of view that we would have been forever lost and undone if infinite wisdom, love, and grace had not been concerned for us. As Romans 5:8 states, "God commended his love toward us in that while we were yet sinners Christ died for us!" These are riches of grace, treasures of wisdom, and exceedingly great shows of his power! This salvation contains such wonderful displays of divine perfections that the angels desire to stoop down and look into it (1 Peter

1:12). How can we look upon other objects with esteem and admiration while this great design of divine wisdom and love is no more admired, esteemed and delighted in by us.

1. One special way of putting honor on God for this great salvation is to entertain high and honorable thoughts of it. God's last and highest end in all his works is his own glory, and it seemed good to the divine wisdom to manifest his glory this way. And he will be *admired* for it throughout the days of eternity. Now none can doubt that those for whom these great things are done should be peculiarly concerned to give him the glory of it. Did the blessed God design to glorify himself in this work or to give occasion to men and angels to do it? How unworthy of us to fail to recognize and praise this great design? Now we shall not do this if we content ourselves with some verbal acknowledgements of God for it, and don't have hearts deeply affected with it and don't admire the divine perfections shining in it... and if we don't view with wonder and praise the glory of his grace and love in the incarnation and humiliation of the Son of God, the glorious discoveries of his holiness, truth, justice, wisdom, and power, and the immense and infinite goodness of God evidenced by it. How justly offended was God with the people of Israel when they lost a sense of his mercy in their deliverance from the Egyptian tyranny, when they did not remember the multitude of his mercies nor the great things he did for them. And yet this was only a temporal mercy and a shadow of this glorious work. Therefore, not to admire God in this would be the height of *ingratitude*. What more could God ever do to

endear himself to us, and engage the highest esteem of him, than what he has already done in this astonishing work of redemption?

2. Admirations of the divine glory will be good evidence of your interest in the privileges of redemption. Those who have shared in this great deliverance from sin and wrath will have high thoughts of their deliverer and of the ways and means by which deliverance had been accomplished. As 1 Peter 2:7 states, "Unto you that believe he is precious." Those to whom Christ is precious do believe. A high valuation of Christ in his person, offices, and benefits is concomitant to true faith and evidence of it. Those who have been led to a spiritual understanding of the glory of the person of Christ, the acceptability of his obedience, the sufficiency of his satisfaction, the glory of divine wisdom in the contrivance and carrying on the work of our redemption, will and do undoubtedly close with it, and depend upon this glorious Savior. Men show their dependance upon created helps by their high thoughts of the sufficiency of them. Such a high esteem of the sufficiency and excellency of Christ will reveal your association with him. The apostle discovered his interest in Christ by his transcendent respect for and esteem of him. Philippians 3:8 says, "I count all things but loss for the excellency of the knowledge of Christ Jesus my Lord." And in this way, the sincere Christian is characterized by his transcendent esteem of Christ and willingness to part with everything for him.

USE III. As the salvation which the gospel reveals is so great and glorious, be exhorted to secure an interest in it.

This is the unquestionable duty of those that have the offer of it made to them. If this is not your serious concern and endeavor, you receive the grace of God in vain and are none the better for its discovery. The apostle tells us in 1 Timothy 1:15, "This is a faithful saying, and worthy of all acceptance, that Christ Jesus came into the world to save sinners." Had this deliverance been a great deal less than it is, it would still have been worthy of acceptance. Had it been only a reprieve from hell for some hundreds of years, or a release from its torment and misery after a certain number of years, this would have been worthy of acceptance. Men are willing to endure a great deal of suffering for a few years of comfort. So how much more worthy is it because it entails total release and discharge from the sufferings of sin forever! When far beyond all this God is pleased to provide a salvation by which we may have not just a partial but a full deliverance from all the effects of sin, and be made partakers of peace and friendship with God, to enjoy all needful spiritual blessings, and to be sharers with angels in the everlasting fruition of God in heavenly glory! This ought to be most earnestly sought after by all that have the offer of it made to them.

1. Consider the absolute necessity of complying with the terms of the gospel and being interested in the salvation that it offers. Men will work hard to attain the conveniences of life. But reason acknowledges it to be wise to take care of things that are necessary that they may have food to eat and clothing to wear. Men usually say they must have these and will stop at nothing to obtain them. And can these be more

necessary than the bread of life or the garments of salvation? What shall become of you if Christ is not a Savior to you? God has not left men to have their choice of several ways by which they may be accepted, justified, and saved. Rather, he has limited it to this: if you don't obtain salvation upon the terms of the gospel there is no hope of being saved at all. There were only two ways proposed to man by which he might obtain eternal life, either by innocence and sinless obedience or by the righteousness of Jesus Christ; either by the works of the law or the grace of Christ appearing in the gospel. The first of these became impossible in man's fallen estate. None that understand themselves or the law can pretend to put in any plea for life upon the terms of the first covenant. The *whole world* is become *guilty* before God, (Rom. 3:19). *By the works of the law shall no flesh be justified* (Gal. 2:16). None of the race of sinful man, no matter how blamelessly, soberly, or conscientiously they may have lived, can put forward any plea for eternal life that might be accepted by God. It is the righteousness of Christ alone that a guilty creature procures absolution and acceptance for him before God; this only can endure the trial of God's tribunal. God never justified any of the sinful children of men upon any other account, nor does he give the least encouragement that he ever will.

2. Consider, the completeness of the salvation that the gospel offers, such as is most suitable to your necessities. There were many hindrances in the way of man's salvation, God was offended and must be satisfied; the law was broken and must be vindicated; Satan had usurped a power over

sinful man as a prisoner and captive to him; the world had gained possession of his heart and affections. All these obstacles had to be overcome. But the wisdom and love of God graciously saw man's necessity and provided a most suitable and complete remedy. Concerning the Lord Jesus Christ, it is said that, "he is able to save to the uttermost all that come unto God by him," (Heb. 7:25). To the uttermost of our needs and the uttermost of our desires. Offended justice was fully satisfied by what Christ suffered, and the authority of the law was maintained. The holiness and wisdom of God was displayed in the obedience and death of the Lord Jesus Christ, so nothing stood in the way of the salvation of a believer. The merit and power of Christ rescued man from the hand of Satan, the power of sin, and the snares of the world (Rom. 16:20) and comforts them against the snares of the world with this encouragement in John 26:33, "Be of good cheer, I have overcome the world." There is in Christ Jesus not only a fulness of merit, but an overflowing fulness of the Spirit to sanctify and preserve us to a state of heavenly glory, as well as to purchase salvation for us. Surely such a savior should be highly acceptable to your souls, and most thankfully embraced.

    3. The clarity of the revelation of gospel light that you enjoy should cause you to desire to get a better understanding of it and the blessings that it offers. God was pleased to instruct the children of Israel in the doctrine of salvation by Jesus Christ by many types and ceremonies which were shadows of good things to come. Their light was glorious when compared to the state of the pagan world, but

obscure in comparison to the New Testament dispensation. As 2 Corinthians 3:6-11 explains, things that were dark before are now made plain. Light has broken forth with great evidence and authority, so that it is said, "light and immortality are brought to light by the gospel," (2 Tim. 1:19). On this account our Savior said to his disciples in Matthew 13:16-17, "Blessed are your eyes for they see, and your ears for they hear. For verily I say unto you that many prophets and righteous men have desired to see these things which ye see, and have not seen them, and to hear these things which ye hear, and have not heard them." Considering these things, we can reasonably expect God's desires for us in this dispensation would include an increased understanding of the glory of Christ in his natures, person, and offices and a heightened interest in this wonderful salvation that he has provided us.

    4. There is a special providence of God directing the dispensation of the gospel, both as to the times and places where it shall be offered. The apostle's journeys were ordered by the Spirit, as noted in Acts 8:26 through 16:7. Now by his gracious designation and choice providences it is brought and laid before you. It may therefore be said to you as was sometime to them, "To you is the word of this salvation sent," (Acts 13:26). You have been blessed with this special mercy; your time is a time of light and grace. An accepted time and a day of salvation! As a result, you have great reason to acknowledge the distinguishing grace of God in this matter toward you, when so many in the world are awash in ignorance, heresies, barbarism, and

superstitions, even in Christianized parts of the world. But especially astonishing is the condescension of God, that he has not contented himself with barely revealing it, but to urge your reception of it with the most proper and forcible arguments. He directs his ambassadors to entreat sinners to receive the offer that is made; as in that wonderful verse in 2 Corinthians 5:20, "As though God did beseech you by us, we pray you in Christ's stead be reconciled to God." The great and glorious God who neither lacks the friendship nor the service of any of his creatures is pleased to become a Suitor for them, to use the most persuasive arguments with them, to pursue their own happiness by receiving the grace provided in Christ. Now let your own judgment and consciences determine whether it is a most becoming and reasonable thing that you should put a due value upon the offer! That you may not be found guilty of receiving the grace of God in vain. God does not offer it to you out of necessity, but out of choice so that both his mercy and your own interest should oblige you to receive it. If you slight God's offers, he can find those that will gladly receive them. As the apostle said to them in Acts 28:28, "The salvation of God is sent unto the Gentiles, and they will hear it." How long have the arms of mercy been stretched out in vain to you? How many calls have been refused? How infrequently have you responded to the Lord's extension of mercy? Shall it still be so? Can you find it in your hearts to wear out divine patience, to trample upon divine mercy, and to refuse your own happiness, to rather hearken to the ensnaring delusions of the grand enemy of your souls, regardless of all the care

God has taken to secure your salvation? Who can express the sin and folly of refusing salvation so graciously provided and so freely offered and brought to your doors? It was this that gave occasion to that passionate lamentation of Christ over Jerusalem, "because they knew not the time of their visitation," (Luke 19:42).

5. Your neglect of salvation will be very sinful and inexcusable. The sinfulness of neglect is manifest in its opposition to the express declaration of the divine will and is aggravated by the light and fulness of grace manifested in the gospel. What more can be desired to persuade and convince the consciences of men of the truth of the gospel and of the sincerity of God in his offer of it, than what God has already done? And how inexcusable then will be your sin if you neglect it? You can't pretend you did not know of it, or that salvation was to be expected in any other way, or that there wasn't sufficient assurance of the truth of the gospel, or that you did not have a reason to look for an interest in the blessings of it. Much less will you be able to plead that you had business of greater weight and necessity to busy your time and thoughts about and therefore had no time to apply yourself to it. Every mouth will be stopped in the great trial. But in that day, sinners will be most of all inexcusable and self-condemned. It is certain that if you can't satisfy your consciences now, you will be much less able to clear yourselves before God hereafter.

Part 4

Proposition IV. How great and glorious is the salvation that the gospel reveals, that is by too many neglected.

The apostle intimates this by the supposition he makes of the fearful hazard that will be the consequence of neglecting it. This is a truth so frequently experienced that there is ground for the prophet's complaint in Isaiah 53:1, "Who hath believed our report?" From one age and generation to another it has been so among those that the gospel has been preached to. This is a dismal proof of the deplorable state of man by the fall, which has not only brought guilt and wrath upon him, but a fearful blindness and obstinacy and a most wretched aversion from God. For though he is perishing for lack of salvation, yet when it is brought to him, and most graciously offered, he does not have a heart to receive it. This gave occasion to those complaints of our Savior in Matthew 23:37, "How often would I have gathered you, and ye would not." Eternal and abundant life was to be found in Christ, but they did not care for it and would not come to Christ for it. This is the spirit of men *still*. Salvation is provided by Christ, revealed in the gospel, offered to men in the ministry, urged upon them by the motions of the Holy Spirit and the voice of their own consciences. But still there remain many who are none the better for it, who obtain no peace or pardon, no grace or comfort by it. This arises from the neglect of it and not receiving the opportunities and offers of the gospel that are afforded them.

Many disregard the offers of the gospel made to them. We read of such in Matthew 22:5, those who when invited to partake in the privileges of the gospel, made light of it. They heard it as a matter of little use and concern to them. There are too many careless and inconsiderate sleepy hearers of the word. They hear as if they had not heard. They don't seriously regard the messages sent them by God from day to day. They don't attend to the things that are spoken regarding their eternal welfare. It is strange to see what ignorance there is in many about the necessary doctrines of salvation they are often taught, and what insensibilities there are in many more regarding the worth of that salvation which the gospel reveals. This happens because they do not mind or weigh the truths that are delivered to them. How many live as if they were only born for time and the interests and pleasures of the present life, and had nothing to do with eternity? They spend their days in pleasure; their lives are a continual diversion from one carnal delight to another. Their thoughts run continually on these things, such that they regard no proposals made to them of things that refer to their eternal safety and welfare. These are utterly *ignorant* of the state their souls are in. A spirit of deep sleep is fallen upon them. They will own that they are sinners; but their being so is no burden nor terror to them. And though they hear of a Savior, and all his glorious sufficiency is set before them to remove their guilt and restore their souls, they give him no thought or consideration.

2. There are also those that don't seriously make it their concern to get a right understanding of the way of salvation which the gospel reveals or to be *interested* in it. They truly neglect salvation that are not concerned to be saved and that don't attempt to understand the terms and method in which it may be obtained. Many have a *superficial knowledge* of the doctrine of the gospel, being all their days educated under it while being negligent in receiving and applying it. They have *no delight* to employ their minds in meditating on it, or to know the Spirit and feel the power of it upon their hearts. They don't get an understanding of the excellency and suitability of it to their condition and determine what importance it is to them, how much the command of God and a respect to their own safety and welfare obliges them to attend to the proposals of it. They do not care that Christ with all his benefits may be theirs, that they may share in the glorious privileges of pardon, peace, holiness, and a title to eternal life by him. Some have a desire to be saved now and then; they may express some concern about it under some awakening truth or providence that they meet with. But for the most part it is a matter of indifference to them. Their minds are intent upon other matters, and they can content themselves to live in a state of estrangement from God without any interest in the graces of his spirit or any well-grounded hope in his promises. That which should be their grand concern and pursued with the greatest application of mind is laid aside, and other things are preferred before it.

Those that purposely delay this grand concern of securing salvation to themselves and leave it as a matter of future care presume their souls are in no present danger. They believe they may safely indulge their security and yield to other designs. They will grant the work of faith to be necessary and say they would not dare die without it; but they do not see a present necessity for it. Just as Felix dealt with his convictions under the apostle's preaching by deferring them to a more convenient season, so they put off this great duty of believing in Christ until some other matters are cleared, or until death is near. They truly neglect the salvation of the gospel in order to improve the season allotted to them for obtaining it.

Then there are those that are under the power of an *unbelieving* heart. It is a fruit of the natural corruption of the heart to discredit and question God's truth as well as to resist his authority. And men are very prone when they hear of the abundant grace of God in Christ towards sinners to question the truth of the report, to doubt whether it is so or not, or to look upon the offers made them as too great to be true. They measure God by themselves and think him prone to revenge and slow to mercy. Their guilt fills them with jealousies and suspicions of God; they see him as one hard to approach, as one whose mercy is with great difficulty obtained from him. They believe they must do some great thing to obtain it and move God to exercise it. They don't see themselves to be people for whom the offer of grace is available, and that it would require too much boldness and arrogance from them to seek it. This is not as common among us as presumption and security, as there are more *presumers* than *despairers*. But still it is the case of many who spend their days in fruitless complaints and dejection of spirit, who consider the authority and divinity of the scriptures and the sufficiency of the grace and power of Christ as though there were not shelter enough under his wings to defend them.

There is an abundance of blamable causes to which neglect of this salvation might be assigned, but I shall only hint at the more general.

1. A prevailing love for some lust. The lusts of men frequently have great control over their affections, partly because these lusts are so closely connected to their corrupt natures and partly because of the many carnal advantages they believe they gain by them. Men's lusts are dear to them. Their importance is represented in Scripture sometimes by a right hand or a right eye. They hide and allow them and will not let them go. Others will ruin their estates, grieve their friends, wound their consciences, and impair their bodies just to hold on to them. And it is from their excessive love for them that many will allow their souls to perish forever. They are not willing that Christ should save them from their sins or that he should exert the power of his grace *to mortify their lusts*. They would be glad to be saved from hell, but they *can't bear* to part from some sweet bosom sins, and the profit or pleasure of these lusts blinds them. They are hardened through the deceitfulness of sin. They could be glad for Christ to pacify their consciences, but they must have their lusts to gratify their corrupt and carnal affections.

They are not willing that Christ should do the whole work of Savior for them, which is in effect to refuse that he should do any part of it. For the receiving of and submitting to Christ in all his offices is an essential condition if we are to partake in the benefit of his sufferings and mediation. Men's natural aversion to sin and their strong and fixed love for their lusts are the reasons why so many neglect and refuse the salvation which the gospel offers them.

2. An inordinate desire for the lawful enjoyments of the world is another cause of this widespread neglect. Worldly comforts are present and favorable to the senses, such things as men desire and taste sweetness in. Therefore, the temptations toward them are all the more forceful. Their cares for the present life make men neglect their future. Things of time are so pressing and urgent that eternal mercies are of little concern. This is represented to us in Luke 14:17-20. It was so then, and still is the great hindrance to men's valuing and receiving Christ. Fears of poverty prevail more upon them than fears of damnation. Desires for grandeur and pomp of living, or to equal or outshine their neighbors in riches and honor, is of more value to them than to have their souls adorned with grace and prepared for glory. Their heads and hands are so full of their worldly plans, and they are so wholly swallowed up in the thoughts and cares about them, that they have no heart or time to think of the state of their souls or to provide for the future welfare of them. They live as if they were born only to mind their present earthly interests only to perish and be forgotten forever after a while like the beasts. For these

reasons, even though they may have *some* convictions of the guilt of sin and the dangerous state of their souls, they quench and suppress these convictions with all these worldly considerations. They can't listen to them until this or the other design and business they have in hand for the world is dispatched. It is the prevalence of this spirit that makes men neglect duties of worship in their families or omit spiritual opportunities that might be for their soul's advantage. This worldly spirit is as much a hindrance to the souls of men in this great duty as any one thing seems to be and it is to be feared as the principal cause of this neglect.

3. It arises also from senseless prejudices which men take up against the way of salvation or the means of the application of it. In Matthew 11:6, our Savior pronounces those blessed who are not *offended* in him. Too many are, and by this they further their own misery. Some take offence at the strict and self-denying terms of the gospel. They are not willing to sell all for the pearl of great price or to part with their lusts. Some reject the strictness of a spiritual life. They would have more liberty than Christ will allow. Christ does not rob men of any lawful liberty, but some desire unlawful liberties. The great objection that many have against Christ is that they will not have him rule over them (Luke 10:27). The laws of Christ are too strict for them. Again, others reject the gospel because they are offended or put off by those who call themselves Christian or are associated with religion. It is no excuse to reject the gospel because some that own him carry it badly, for we are forewarned that there will be hypocrites in the visible church. The laws of Christ

give no allowance for the misconduct of believers, but too many nourish a base opinion of religion for this reason and reject the proposals of the gospel. Some are prejudiced against the instruments by whom the offer of salvation is brought to them either because of some natural or moral imperfection they object to, their lack of means or infirmities, or some personal grudge they have taken up against them. They don't regard the message because they slight and dis-esteem the messenger that brings it. Thus, the Jews stumbled at the outward meanness of Christ and the apostles, because they were men of no note and fame in the world.

  4. Neglect of this salvation may also come from the influence of bad examples. One's neglect and carelessness are a temptation to another. There are sometimes seasons of fresh and plentiful effusions of the Spirit of God upon a place, and at these times many will be pressing into the kingdom of God. The zeal of some provokes others, which helps to awaken and quicken one another. But again, there are times of great deadness, and at such times men harden one another. They are quick to reason with themselves that this or that one thinks they may disregard the gospel without any hazard, especially when those do so whom they esteem to be men of prudence and whose judgment they value. This is a temptation to think that if it were a matter of such dangerous consequence to neglect, such persons would never do so. Men are very much led by example, especially by those of the same standing with them. This is a temptation to many young people. They see their friends

as carefree and unconcerned about such matters and are thereby encouraged in their sins and in the neglect of the grace offered them by Christ.

5. It is neglected by many because of the spirit that is in men naturally, and indeed universally, inclining them to seek justification by their *own* works. Every man comes into the world under the obligation of the *covenant of works* and naturally runs to it for life. A spirit of self-love is apt to blind these men so that they can't see their own defects. They had rather have a few rags of their own than ask for Christ to clothe them in the robes of his righteousness. And sometimes they seek their own justification out of ignorance, not understanding the excellency and sufficiency of Christ's righteousness or its acceptability to God to the end for which it is proposed. They do not understand the glorious design of God to exalt his grace in the free justification of a sinner by the imputation of Christ's righteousness alone, without the works of the law. This was the case of the Jews at the first preaching of the gospel in Romans 10:3. No doctrine was more despised by them than this of justification by the righteousness of Christ through faith. And it is this doctrine that the great enemies of God's grace have attempted to obscure and resist.

6. This neglect also arises from the influence and activity of Satan to blind and darken the minds of men and set them against this duty. To this the apostle refers in 2 Corinthians 4:3-4, "If our gospel is hid, it is hid to them that are lost, in whom the God of this world hath blinded the minds of them that believe not." Satan is the great promoter

of all sin, the enemy of all righteousness. But he especially engages himself and uses his primary power to harden men in unbelief and keep them from closing with Christ upon the terms of the gospel, and he uses every method available to him to do so. He convinces men that they need not trouble themselves about a better righteousness and tempts them to embrace an image of faith instead of true saving faith.

USE I. This shows why we should concern ourselves that the salvation provided by Christ and offered in the gospel is so undervalued. The mercy and grace of God, the privileges of the gospel, the salvation herein revealed and proposed, and the accompanying blessings and promises of a spiritual and eternal nature are of highest importance to the souls of men. Christ offers reconciliation with God, remission of sin, redemption from the curse of the law, a title to eternal life and all the blessings that eternity with God in a state of heavenly glory can afford. But how few comparatively value it, regard it, and are concerned to have an *interest* in it. The glad tidings of the gospel grow stale and common in our times; it is the world and worldly enjoyments and interests that men are inquiring after and busying themselves with. The favor of God and eternal life seem to be small and inconsiderable when compared to the great expectations they have from the world. The prevailing of such a spirit calls for great concern on several accounts.

1. On account of the greatness of the sin. This sin has the greatest ingratitude and unkindness in it, for it is a sin against the freest love and richest mercy that ever was manifested to the world. The apostle in Hebrews 10:28-29

addresses this by way of a comparison taken from sins against the law. The bold transgressions of the law were punished with the death of the transgressor. The apostle adds "how much more!" when considering the voluntary transgressions against the gospel. And in proportion, neglecting the grace tendered in the gospel will bring an answerable degree of punishment, even God's divine wrath to the uttermost! What wonderful love was it that when the whole world was found guilty before God, and nothing but certain death could have been expected by any of the sinful children of men, that the kindness and love of God appeared instead. He sent his own son in the likeness of sinful flesh to be a surety and sacrifice for us! He was made to be made sin and a curse for us, to take upon himself the obligation we were under to discharge it in our stead, by offering up himself to make atonement for our sin. And not only to procure deliverance from sin and all the penal effects of it, but to purchase and offer eternal life and glory in the world to come. To consider that God should single you out to be the subjects of these offers, what astonishing grace is this! How great then is the ingratitude of those who slight, disregard and neglect this offer of salvation? That you should carry yourself so towards God as if his image and favor were things of little worth! And regarding Christ, as if he spent his life and endured his sufferings for things of such little value and account that they are not even worth your esteem and reception! How much are men offended when their favors are slighted. And how much more may the blessed God be, when such rich and glorious offers as he makes are not regarded by the children of men.

2. On account of the sad effects sin is attended with, even in this world, and those judgments that it brings with it. When the Jews rejected Christ, God destroyed that nation by astonishing judgments. For a long time now, God has been pleading with this land, showing his displeasure by many awful providences. Undoubtedly there are many things which God has been provoked by unrighteousness, oppression, fraud, falsehood, intemperance, uncleanness, profaning his sabbath, murmurings, pride, and other evils that too frequently break out. But one primary reason for God's provocation with us is not valuing and receiving the grace of Christ offered in the gospel. The jealousy of God has been provoked because we have idolized and preferred worldly pleasures and trophies before Christ. Those who neglect this great salvation are to be found in all our towns, from one end of the land to another. It is the prevailing sin of our day. The minds and thoughts of many are possessed with other things. The general cry is, "what shall we eat, what shall we drink?" and not, "what must we do to be saved?" If men understood and considered what a great blessing salvation from sin is, and received the help offered them by Christ for that end, they would not indulge and cherish sin as much as they do. But this neglect of the grace of Christ and overvaluing the things of the world disposes men to acts of unrighteousness, to defraud, to break their promises, to be uncharitable and covetous. This sin not only produces an abundance of other sins but keeps men from the

only remedy from all sin. Further, it is in its nature most vile, being in direct opposition to God's greatest design, to exalt the glory of his grace towards sinners by Jesus Christ.

3. In regard to, the certain danger those who neglect salvation face in terms of eternal judgments. It is a sin that not only provokes God to shorten men's lives, to put an end to their opportunities of gospel light and grace, and to bring many difficulties upon them in this world, but it will also bring unavoidable destruction to them in the world to come. If this way of salvation is neglected, there is no remedy and no way to escape remaining for guilty sinners. God has provided no other sacrifice for sin. And if you continue impenitent and unbelieving, that most certainly will cut you off from any claim to the benefits of Christ. He that does not believe in the Son *shall not see life* (John 3:36). Except men repent, they *must* perish. Unbelief is eminently the mortal sin that damns sinners and leaves them to experience judgment without mercy. It is not the *preparation* of a sovereign remedy that cures a disease, but the *application* of it. The righteousness and spirit of Christ, however sufficient for the ends to which they are provided, convey no pardon to any soul that is not by faith united to him. It is not from any defect of mercy in God or merit in Christ that so many perish, but from their obstinate refusal of it; that *precious blood which speaks better things than the blood of Abel* (Heb. 12:24), calls for mercy to believing sinners and for vengeance and damnation upon the heads of the unbelieving and impenitent. How sad is the fact that the last end for so many of the miserable children of Adam will be to perish forever?

Temporal miseries that some endure are very sorrowful; the spiritual judgments that others undergo are more sorrowful. But eternal evils immeasurably exceed both.

4. On the account that their opportunities for avoiding the miseries they are in danger of, and obtaining the mercies offered them, will quickly be gone. As Paul says in 2 Corinthians 6:1, "Behold! Now is the accepted time, now is the day of salvation!" And "He calls upon them to hear his voice while it is called today," (Heb. 3:7). God lets men know that his hourglass of patience is continually running down and will soon run out. The opportunity sinners have to embrace the gospel is *continually* eluding them. Some are already at an advanced age and with respect to nature can't expect many more chances. Others by continuing in sin have increased their natural obstinance. Others have contracted evil habits, or brought themselves under spiritual judgments, and have provoked God to put a limit on them. Such loss was the consideration of our Savior that caused him to weep over Jerusalem, (Luke 19:44), "that she knew not the time of her visitation." It is a very woeful consideration to see multitudes of mankind riding the stream of time into the ocean of eternity, all the while not considering where they are going or how they will experience that eternal state!

USE II. Examine yourself to see whether you are guilty of this sin of neglecting the great salvation which is revealed and offered to you in the gospel. Few acknowledge their guilt in this matter, and many deceive themselves because of some common effects of conviction or comfort that the gospel had upon them, such that they create false hopes that all shall be well.

The great question I would challenge you to ask of your soul is whether you have been brought thankfully to receive the blessings offered, and heartily to submit to the terms propounded in the gospel? Regardless of how honorably men speak of the gospel and its privileges, if their hearts are not bowed to consent to the offers it makes and submit to the duties it requires, they neglect it. A few particulars are offered here for your help in this trial.

1. If you have received the grace offered in the gospel, you value the privileges of it. Both Christ himself and the benefits of Christ are precious to believers. The privileges of salvation are various, but to value them all, or indeed to rightly value any, is one distinguishing character of true believers. Peace with God is one of the privileges of the gospel. Carnal men would be glad that God would not hurt them. But in terms of any real esteem of his favor, rejoicing in his friendship, or valuing his presence or fellowship with him, they are strangers to this. A gracious soul does value these benefits, however, and accordingly prefers the favor of God, "above the increases of corn and wine," (Psa. 4:5-7). And "accounts his loving kindness to be better than life," (Psa. 63:2). The friendship of God is more to them than the favor of all the world. The sense they have of the excellency of it is the great inducement to a holy walk before God. And access to God, as to a father in Christ, that they may come and pour out their hearts to him in all their straits and necessities, is a privilege which gracious souls highly esteem

and gratefully appreciate. Here their approach to God is not that of slavish fear but of love. They *delight* to come into God's presence that they may express a sense of his grace towards them and may obtain further manifestations and experiences of it. Another privilege believers have in Christ which they highly value is deliverance from the reigning power and dominion of sin (Rom. 6:14). This is a principal part of that liberty which they enjoy by Christ at present, that by his Spirit he enables them to mortify the deeds of the body (Rom. 8:13). They are made partakers of a new nature by the Spirit of Christ working in them which inclines them not only to avoid and resist, but to hate sin, and to love and prize holiness. And as they are in consideration of the death of Christ and his design in redemption to engage their hearts against sin, so they have recourse to the spirit of Christ for direction and help in the course of their duty, and for assistance in their conflicts and temptations. And knowing that the salvation which is begun in them shall in due time be perfected, they gladly pursue the perfection of holiness and abolition of sin. Further, even now while they are burdened with the cares of this world and remain in this earthly body, they rejoice in Christ as one that in due time will bring them to full and complete victory over sin (Rom. 7:24-25).

    2. If you have received the salvation of the gospel, you will discover your best and sweetest comforts from its hopes. The apostle says that believers, "rejoice in hope of the glory of God," (Rom. 5:2). It is our duty even to rejoice in God on account of the present effects of his goodness that

we enjoy. But the chief joy of a believer is in God through Christ, and in the hopes of that perfect and satisfying blessedness that shall be enjoyed with God in a state of heavenly glory. These promises are their songs in the house of their pilgrimage; these lighten their burdens and relieve their trials and distresses here. They reckon with the apostle in Romans 8:18 that "the sufferings of this present time are not worthy to be compared with the glory which shall be revealed in them." They are often refreshing themselves with the meditations of the greatness and goodness and certainty of the promises of God, the mercy and love that has made such glorious preparations for such unworthy creatures as we are. We are therefore waiting and longing for the day of redemption and groaning under the unsuitable nature of our hearts to the glory and blessedness of the state that is prepared for us. The disposition of the heart is as much discovered by what it rejoices in the hope of, as in the possession of. Carnal men show the states of their hearts by the carnal expectations that they feed themselves with, as well as by *what they enjoy* (Luke 12:19-20). Gracious souls discover the heavenly focus of their hearts by seeking the things that are above and groaning after the perfecting of their redemption. Carnal men may desire heaven as their *refuge* when they can be here no longer, but godly men desire it as their *inheritance*.

3. If you have received the salvation of the gospel, it will be your serious aim and endeavor to walk worthy of the Lord. It is a vile abuse of the gospel to take encouragement from it to continue in sin on the hope that the mercy of God

and merit of Christ will win out. God had quite another design in revealing his grace to sinners in the gospel. We are told in Titus 2:11-12 that, "the grace of God which bringeth salvation hath appeared to all men, teaching us that denying ungodliness and worldly lusts, we should live soberly righteously and godly in this present world." Those who understand the truth as it is in Christ Jesus see a glory in this method of divine grace, as it carries the strongest arguments against sin and the most forcible inducements to holiness and purity and righteousness. As they have been made sensible of their misery by reason of the power as well as the guilt of sin, they know it is their privilege to benefit from the offer and promise of grace in Christ to take away the power of sin and to enable and assist them to walk in newness of life. Therefore the Scripture frequently insists upon such signs of faith as sure evidence of it. Those who are made partakers of life in Christ discover it in righteousness, truth, and a care of universal holiness in the course of their lives. Consider therefore, is this your spirit? Do you see a beauty in holiness? Do you love the divine law because of the purity of it? Do you apply God's promises, ordinances, and providences to the advancement of holiness in your hearts and lives? Are you truly thankful for any advance and progress in it? After giving in to temptation do you run to Christ in repentance, seeking his pardoning mercy and to renew your watchfulness against sin and a more strict dependance upon him, that his power might rest on you, and his strength be perfected in your weakness? This is the spirit of believers.

USE III. To advise all who have neglected the salvation that has been offered them in the gospel now to embrace it. Listen to God's calling for your present comfort and future happiness. That caution of the apostle in Hebrews 12:15 deserves consideration, "looking diligently lest any man fail of the grace of God." Every man, in particular, needs to be concerned that he does not fail to gain an interest in the grace of God or come short of salvation. The revelation of the grace of God to sinners in the gospel is in itself a mercy. But if the doctrine of the gospel is not believed and understood, nor the mercies it offers received, it will eventually prove an aggravation of sin and a heightening of judgment.

I shall now offer a few words of advice.

1. Determine to shake off presumption and a false sense of security, because herein is salvation is so much neglected. Men presume they have time enough before them. They presume upon the patience of God, the continuance of means, the assistances of the Spirit, all which are utterly uncertain and not at their command. They presume upon their good purposes and resolutions without understanding the deceitfulness and desperate wickedness of their own hearts. They have no heart to be concerned about their eternal welfare, but rather content themselves either with lazy desires or superficial and formal duties. Abandon these presumptions! Conclude that now is the season of hope because you do not know when God will put an end to your time or suspend the influences of his Spirit.

2. Gain knowledge about your absolute and present need of this salvation that is offered to you. A sense of need quickens endeavor. God has given you many advantages to know this – by his word, by the voice of conscience, by his providences, by the confessions and experiences of others. You are capable of understanding and passing a true judgment upon your state and actions, to see the many sins you have been guilty of in the course of your lives, to see the truth of the threatening and curse of the law that lies upon you and stands in force against you, your utter insufficiency to fulfill your need for righteousness or to bear the penalty of it, to make any compensation for sin, to give to God any ransom for your souls, or to offer anything to God that may be a price for eternal life. So, unless a Savior intervenes for you, you must indeed perish, and it is altogether uncertain how soon that will be.

3. Labor to understand the sufficiency of the Savior and the salvation that the gospel reveals, as well as the just and honorable terms upon which it is offered. The principal means God has appointed to be used to bring you to a knowledge of these things are diligent hearing and searching into the word of God and earnest supplications to God for his Spirit to instruct you. The word reveals Christ and provides the terms of salvation. The Spirit opens the understanding to see the truth and glory of the things revealed (John 5:39 and 16:14). There you are informed of the natures, person, and offices of Christ: how mighty he is to save even to the uttermost those that come to God by him. It shows us the completeness of his satisfaction, the

acceptability of his sufferings, the prevalence of his intercession, the riches of his grace and mercy, his readiness to receive and undertake for believing sinners that find an utter inability to save themselves. He imposes terms that are not only just but honorable and gracious. He requires no part of the satisfaction due to the law from the sinner himself, but an entire dependance upon what he has made available by his obedience and sufferings. He simply requires that you leave your sins through repentance and return to your duty to God by an entire dedication of yourselves, soul, body, time, interests, and affections to his glory and praise. He encourages and promotes this with his great and precious promises of eternal life and happiness as your reward at last. Surely you should be ashamed if you neglect so great a salvation.

Part 5

Proposition V. The neglect of this great salvation will expose men to great and unavoidable misery.

The reception and entertaining of it will secure the greatest happiness and the choicest blessings to the children of men, and the neglect of it will bring on the sorest and heaviest condemnation. This is a plain truth from the words of our text. The apostle's question supposes the strongest negation – there will be no escaping the severest vengeance from God if the salvation offered in the gospel is neglected and refused. Listen to 1 Peter 4:17, "What shall the end of them be that obey not the gospel of God?" How miserable and dreadful it will be, he does not say but leaves it to their own thoughts and consciences to judge. The plagues and miseries that shall fall upon the most abominable among the heathen shall not be comparable to those who shall be found guilty of despising and sinning against the remedy offered in the gospel (Matt. 11:22).

That their misery will be exceedingly great appears from the nature, quality, and kind of it in the following particulars.

1. They will have none of their sins pardoned but must expect to answer for, and bear the guilt of them all. Whenever the salvation offered in the gospel is received rightly, remission of sins is one happy effect of it. Remission of sin always follows true faith and repentance (Acts 3:19,

10:43). But on the other hand, unbelieving and impenitent sinners have the guilt of all their sins lying upon them. There's *no* remission of sin without the blood of Christ; and without faith in Christ, there is no interest in his blood, and consequently no pardon. Sinners stand guilty before God of numerous sins, but however many there are, they are all chargeable to them. They may have forgotten the abundance of them, but God has *not* forgotten even one of them; they are laid up in store with him and sealed up among his treasures (Deut. 32:34). The Scripture is plain as to this, that none of their sins are pardoned, nor shall be while they abide in unbelief. As John 3:18 clearly states, "He that believeth not is condemned already, because he hath not believed on the name of the only begotten Son of God." And John 8:24, "If ye believe not that I am he, ye shall die in your sins." Now this is a very dreadful misery to have the guilt of all your sins lying upon you; to be liable to answer at the bar of God (as shortly you must) for every sin you have ever committed. The guilt of sin is a heavy burden. The very thought that God would bring them to judgment to answer for the sins they have committed has terrorized many, but when sin comes indeed to be charged to sinners' accounts, it will be unspeakably worse.

(1.) Because then sinners will have a clearer sight of their sins than they have now. Sinners will then have a fuller discovery of the nature, number, and extent of their sins. Here they see but a few of them, and even those who have the fullest conviction of sin don't see them all. There are multitudes of vain thoughts, idle words, omissions of duty, commissions of evil, that they took no notice of or have now slipped their memories. But then there will be a full discovery of them all; they will be judged for all things they have done in the body. Ungodly sinners shall be convinced of all the ungodly deeds, all the evil they have both done and spoken. Jude 15, "God will bring every work into judgment," and Ecclesiastes 12:14, the judgment will be particular both as to people and things. Not one of your sins escapes his knowledge, nor will any of them be forgotten. Then God will make good that word in Psalm 50:21, "but I will reprove thee, and set them in order before thine eyes." And what a dreadful amazing sight it will be for a man to have all his sins *set in order* before him. Conscience will then be filled with light and power and will freely testify for God and against the sinner. It will remind him of his sins and the aggravating circumstances of them. There may be thousands of things that they never saw or believed to be sins that will then be produced against them.

(2.) Then men will have another way of seeing the terror and majesty of God against whom they have sinned than they have now. Many now have slight thoughts of God's power and wrath and are therefore bold to sin. They understand precious little about the power of his anger and the dreadfulness of his wrath but rather assume that God is like them. But when God allows his greatness and majesty and the terror of his wrath to break through, the very sight of it will be intolerable to sinful creatures; they will not be able to bear it but will wish rather to be buried under mountains and dashed in pieces with rocks than to have to face their offended judge (Rev. 6:17). Then they will see and own the truth of what is said in Hebrews 10:31, "it is a fearful thing to fall into the hands of the living God."

(3.) There will be no hope left that they shall ever be pardoned. Even under the greatest distress of conscience that sinners have experienced, there has been this to moderate them, that there has at least been a possibility of pardon, the thought that perhaps God might give repentance. And many who have been under deep distress of spirit, have afterwards had experience of his grace to their abundant support and comfort. But there is no such expectation for those that die in their sins, that continue in their unbelief and neglect of Christ. Their day of grace is over; mercy is done with them. They have no more invitations by a Savior; the patience of God is come to its utmost end with them, and that wrath which they were so long preparing is now executed and has actually seized them. Now, the hopelessness of their condition renders it inexpressibly woeful! There is no hope of forgiveness! No more sacrifice for sin!

2. They must look to bear the wrath and curse of God which belongs to the transgression of the law. Guilt and wrath are inseparable companions. They who have no interest in the promises must expect the execution of the threatening. They who are not saved will be damned (Mark 16:16, John 3:36). They who don't hear that gracious sentence from Christ in Matthew 25:34, "Come ye blessed of my Father," must hear that of verse 41, "Depart ye cursed into everlasting fire!" He who dreams of a middle state between

these two dreams in vain. Those who neglect the salvation which the gospel offers will have nothing to secure them from the dreadful wrath of God. The Lord Jesus Christ will be no advocate for them: he will enter no plea for them, nor will it be in the power of any creature – angels or men – to do anything for their relief. To be sure, the wrath of God due for sin is an intolerable burden; no misery can be compared with this. As the love and favor of God is a privilege that is inconceivably great, so the wrath and anger of God is a misery proportionately dreadful. Who knows the power of his anger? (Psa. 90:11), and, "Who can stand before thine indignation? Who can abide in the fierceness of thine anger?" (Nahum 1:6). Much can be said here concerning the horror of God's anger in the punishments that it shall inflict on sinners. The guilty sinner is deprived at once of all his comforts and all his hopes. He has neither any natural nor spiritual good; all his enjoyments, friends, pleasures, and hopes with which he occupied himself while he lived are now at an end; and he will not have so much as a drop of water to comfort him. As none can describe the blessedness of a soul encircled in the arms of divine love, so none can express the misery of a soul eternally separated from God, confined to the company of devils and the inextinguishable flames of divine wrath!

3. It is beyond question that there will be degrees of punishment in hell, for the judge of all the earth will do right. There shall be an impartial trial: men shall be judged according to their general state (redeemed or damned) and according to their individual sins. This is made clear in Luke

12:47-48. That servant who knew his lord's will and did not prepare himself, neither did according to his will, shall be beaten with many stripes. And the more knowledge and love a person has abused, the more their guilt will be enhanced and the more severe their punishment will be. They will suffer more from their own consciences in the terrible accusations and reproaches that they will bring against themselves. The reflections of conscience upon the light they had, the warnings they were given, the offers that were made to them, the strivings of the spirit that they were sometimes under, will all be inexpressibly distressing to them. They will suffer more than others from the devils who will be their tormentors as well as fellow-sufferers. They who now tempt them to sin and to neglect the means of salvation, will then harass them with it and will be ready to remind them of the grace they neglected. Even Christ himself will appear in greater terror towards them than others. He will make them keenly aware by the splendor of his majesty what a glorious person they slighted and despised.

The more mercy men have had and abused in this world, the more wrath they must expect to feel in the world to come. It will be a dreadful aggravation of the misery of such to remember how near they were to the kingdom of heaven and what base things they forfeited it for. Then sinners will confess that the Scripture is right when it calls them fools.

2. Why is the neglect of the gospel such a fearful thing?

(1.) Because it is an abuse of the greatest love and mercy that God *ever* manifested to the world. The Scripture speaks of the love of God in the gift of Christ as transcendent and superlative (John 3:16; 1 John 4:10). God shows great mercy to man in giving them food and clothing and other necessaries and comforts of life. But infinite love shines forth in the gift of Christ. God had nothing greater and better to give to the world than his own Son, an only son most dear to him, one in whom he took the highest pleasure and satisfaction; a Son that was the brightness of his glory and the express image of his person. To give him to endure such sufferings, to submit to such a state of humiliation and abasement as he was pleased to do, for our sakes to bear the curse that we might have the blessing! To be made sin that we might partake of his righteousness! To die that we might live! For us that could never repay him! To make a free offer of this salvation, yea to repeat the offer maybe hundreds of thousands of times to sinners, and yet all the while to have this glorious Savior despised, this great salvation trampled upon and slighted, as if every trifle, vanity, or lust were more desirable, this must necessarily provoke the heaviest wrath. If men cannot understand the worth and glory of a Savior, how to set a value upon this wonderful wisdom, grace, and love of God that has appeared by way of salvation and the blessed privileges of it, still God knows the worth of these things and how to establish a proportionate punishment for the neglect of it. God has sometimes severely censured those that have despised his servants. Much more may it be expected that he will be severe to those who don't reverence his Son.

(2.) Because such are guilty of refusing the only remedy. This is the last and only refuge or means of relief that God has provided for man's restoration to his image and favor since his apostacy from God. We read in Romans 8:3-4, "For what the law could not do in that it was weak through the flesh, God sending his own son in the likeness of sinful flesh, and for sin condemned sin in the flesh, that the righteousness of the law might be fulfilled in us." When Adam the sponsor and surety of the first covenant failed to obtain life, and men through the loss of the divine image were so weakened and disabled that they could not answer their obligation to it, God was pleased to substitute the Lord Jesus Christ to procure pardon and life by a *new covenant*. But if this way of salvation by Jesus Christ is rejected and slighted, God has made no provision for another. God has laid out the treasures of his wisdom and love in providing this way. Grace and mercy toward sinners have been glorified in as high a degree as we can suppose possible that they should. God has no other son to give to die in the sinners' stead, and death is essential to satisfy man's transgressions against the law for without the shedding of blood, there is no remission. All the blood of beasts shed before the great sacrifice of Christ was offered was insufficient to wash away sin. How can it be thought that satisfaction could be made by any mere creature, when the guilt is against both the law and the gospel too? What could ever atone for contempt of the blood of the Son of God? God has provided no remedy, nor is it in the power of the sinner themselves to provide any. Therefore, their destruction is certain and unavoidable. Finally, the rivers of tears shed by condemned sinners in hell will never be able to quench its flames.

(3.) The certainty of this truth is evident because the justice of God requires it. The blessed God has resolved that he will glorify his Son. The word has gone out of his mouth, and shall not be reversed, that every knee shall bow to him. The whole world shall be either the triumphs of his grace or justice. The Scripture contains an abundance of convictions against unbelievers. It tells us they shall be damned, that they shall never see life, that the wrath of God abides on them, etc. Now these threatenings proceed from a God of invariable truth, unspotted justice, and almighty power, and will surely be accomplished. A secret hope is often nourished in the hearts of sinners that God will not be so strict and severe as to execute his threatenings on them, or if he does, he will not do so in such a terrible a manner as he has threatened. But these hopes are presumptuous and ungrounded. God has given no reason for sinners to build such hopes upon. His threatenings are not rash and sudden determinations as those of man often are. Rather, they are a sanction of the gospel covenant, which God in his eternal wisdom and counsel has determined and established, and therefore will not go back from. God is unalterably just and true in his threatenings as well as in his promises. "He is not a man that he should lie, or the son of man that he should repent," (James 1:15). There is no ground for expectation that God will alter his mind, or that he would ever lack the power to execute his threatenings. Besides, the sufferings of Christ are a convincing proof of the truth of them. God did not spare him when sin was imputed to him; it was necessary that he should drink the bitter cup of divine wrath that the justice and truth of God might be glorified. And if justice would not spare the Son of God, neither will it spare guilty sinners.

These things should be sufficient to confirm the truth before us, that the destruction of those who neglect the salvation offered in the gospel will be certain and unavoidable.

USE I. This truth may evidence the fearful blindness that many sinners are under, who neglect the salvation offered to them by Jesus Christ in the gospel. It is evident from this, because there will be no possibility of escaping God's wrath and vengeance if this salvation is neglected. This way of salvation which the gospel propounds by Jesus Christ is so suitable to the state of fallen man, so accommodated to answer all his necessities and to relieve him under all his wants and fears; so safe a way, and a way wherein so much of the grace, love, and wisdom of God has appeared, that its own excellency may justly recommend it to all to whom the offer is made. But when, together with this, there is such an unavoidable certainty of misery to all who neglect it, one might justly expect that every man should be most deeply concerned to secure an interest in it and use his utmost diligence to make it his own. But alas! What carelessness and indifference do many manifest in this matter! As if it were a thing of little weight or worth, that they might do well enough in the neglect of it. The apostle explains the reason behind such behavior in 2 Corinthians 4:3-4, were not men under fearful blindness and strong delusions from the god of this world, it could not neglect such mercies. This may be further manifested,

(1.) In that they act so contrary to what they profess to be their interest. It is a thing which men generally, if not universally, acknowledge to be necessary to take care of the salvation of their souls and provide for a future happiness, that if Christ is not their surety and Savior, they are miserable, and that the life and safety of their souls depend upon their faith in Christ and repentance towards God. And yet they act as if they loved death and could be contented to risk damnation. Though a Savior is offered them, they neglect or defer *receiving* him. Were they not under a strange infatuation blinded with the love of sin or the love of the world, it would not make sense that they should hazard their souls and run the risk of perishing forever, especially when they know their opportunities are continually passing from them, and they do not know how soon God may put an end to them.

(2.) In that this is the only way in which there is any hope of obtaining salvation. The word of God assures us that as there is one God, so there is one mediator between God and men, and only one. Foolish men have multiplied mediators as well as gods; but God only appointed One, and it is through him alone that salvation is attainable as Acts 4:12 notes, "Neither is there salvation in any other, for there is no other name given among men by which we must be saved." God never saved any of the children of men upon any other account, and there is no reason to expect he ever will. It must be known that heaven is the Lord's, and he may give it to whom he will and upon whatever terms he will. But our Savior tells us in John 14:6, "that he is the way, the truth, and life, and that no man comes to the Father but by him." You must take this way *or perish forever*. They who will not have heaven upon Christ's terms must go without it. When the truth is this clear, it is a most strange delusion they are under who neglect it.

(3.) God has given clear and evident proofs of the certainty of this way of salvation as can reasonably be desired and is willing to bestow it upon the terms propounded in the gospel. Therefore, none can pretend a lack of sufficient reason for encouragement to believe. God in his word plainly shows men what their sinful, helpless, and undone condition is and how impossible it is for them to get righteousness and life by the law. He has also plainly discovered the sufficiency of the satisfaction that Christ made, that he is well pleased with him, and that it was a way of his own contriving. In other words, God sanctified him and sent him into the world (John 10:36). He makes it known that the blood of Christ cleanses from all sin (John 1:7). His satisfaction was fully commensurate with the demands of the law and justice of God. Believers have the sure word and promise of God to depend upon in this matter, yea he has confirmed it by his oath to this end (as the apostle assures in Hebrews 6:17-18) "that the heirs of promise might have strong consolation." God formerly confirmed his word by miraculous works, and still confirms it by many supernatural effects: in awakening, quieting, and comforting the consciences of sinners, filling them with joy unspeakable, and sanctifying their hearts. As the truth of the gospel has been so fully confirmed and is so generally acknowledged, for men to be careless about the salvation it offers surely arises from the blinding and hardening power of sin as well as the delusions imposed upon them by the great adversary of their souls.

USE II. To awaken and reprove those who neglect this great salvation. I urge all who are not seriously and deeply concerned to have their hearts brought to a full compliance with the terms upon which this salvation is offered to abandon their sinful ways, to renounce a dependance upon their own righteousness, and to commit their souls in a way of believing unto the Lord Jesus Christ, as the gospel requires. I shall mention a few things here, to promote the awakening and conviction of such people.

Consider 1. How much contempt of the grace and mercy and condescension of God you are guilty of, by neglecting Christ and the salvation he offers to you? The offers of salvation that are made to sinners are fruits of free and undeserved grace. God had no need of man's friendship or service. He had just right by the law to have glorified himself in the executions of his justice upon man. Nevertheless, it pleased him in his sovereign mercy to provide and reveal a way of salvation, in which he would discover his own perfections and provide for the happiness of man. And as the apostle here informs us, he sent his own Son to work out this salvation for us and to publish it to us. It is that which began to be spoken to us by the Lord. The ever-blessed Lord Jesus Christ was willing to come himself from the bosom of his Father to purchase salvation. Now the greatness of the person sent upon this great errand and design carries the greater obligation in it to all to receive the offer and heightens the sin in the refusal of it. God was justly offended with the Jews that they despised his servants, and expected that surely they would reverence his Son when he sent him among them (Matthew 21:57). The fuller and clearer the revelations of divine grace are to men, the greater assurance God gives of his readiness to accept them and bestow salvation in this way. So naturally, there is also the greater contempt in the neglect and refusal of it. When the children of Israel did not hearken to the law of God delivered by angels at Mount Sinai, this was a contempt of God's authority. But it is a much greater contempt to disobey the gospel which was preached by Christ himself. In the one, God is despised when speaking by his servants, in the other by his Son. There has been a great deal of contempt cast upon God by sinners in all ages. They undervalue his goodness, slight his threatening, trample upon his authority, and walk contrary to his commands which gave occasion to that cry of the psalmist in Psalm 10:13, "therefore does the wicked contemn God!" It is an unreasonable and injurious thing that they should do so; but in this case the contempt rises higher, because not only his authority which requires men to obey the gospel is despised, but his grace and love are *slighted* and *undervalued*.

Consider 2. The inexpressible wrong you do to your own souls. Nature teaches men to love themselves, to seek their own good, and especially notes a due concern for the best part of themselves, their souls. But they that neglect a Savior disregard and undervalue their own souls, which means, by default, they love death. They bring the most certain and inexpressible misery upon their own souls. They cut themselves off from any hope of acceptance with God and any title to a blessed immortality and bring upon themselves certain and unavoidable misery. They can have no pardon of sin, no peace with God, no hope in the promises, no privilege of access to him. These are all obtained by Christ and communicated only for his sake and upon his account to believers. They deprive themselves also of that which is their beauty, their honor, their life; even that holiness and sanctification which is a main part of the salvation which Christ invites sinners to come to him for. If you have received Christ as Savior, the Spirit of holiness is his special gift to you. He saves his people from their sins. He enlightens their minds, renews their wills, purifies their hearts, and conveys and cherishes all spiritual life in them. Now can you be content to be an utter stranger to all true holiness? To live under the tyranny of Satan and reign of sin, to have a soul utterly unserviceable to God while you live, and unfit and unworthy of any fellowship with God when you die? It must be this way if the gracious offer that Christ makes is rejected and slighted.

Consider 3. You oppose, and as much as lies in you, frustrate the main design that God has been carrying on from the beginning of the world. The work of redemption is one of the great and most glorious works of God which has been upon his heart before the foundations of the world, by which he designed to raise eternal honor and glory to himself and to bring about the greatest good to his elect. The means of effecting this is by bringing men to repentance and faith in the Lord Jesus Christ. This is that which God calls men to. The great duty he urges men to is not to receive the grace of God in vain, and it is in vain if his end is not attained. When men act contrary to God's designed ends, one may reasonably conclude that it is very offensive to him, as on the other hand it is pleasing to him when his end is attained. In fact, we read that our Savior rejoiced in spirit upon the report the disciples brought him of the success of their ministry (Luke 10:21). We also read that there is joy in heaven upon a sinner's repentance (Luke 15:7, 10). Heaven rings with joy at the report that God is glorified and a soul is rescued from *destruction*. Further, it is a matter of great joy and refreshing to those whom God sends to urge men to be reconciled to God. When they see the glory of God advanced in the salvation of men, then they shall be able to give up their account with joy. And at another time you read of Christ's being grieved because of the hardness of men's hearts (Mark 8:5) and the fact that they did not believe despite the evident proofs that he gave of his divinity. Now will you grieve and displease this ever-blessed God in crossing him in an end so gracious and so glorious, where your own welfare is entwined so with his honor? Will you rather choose to gratify your lusts and please the devil that would destroy you, than to pour out your souls in earnest cries that his grace may be effective in bringing your hearts to comply with the duty that the gospel requires of you?

Consider 4. By neglecting the grace offered to you in the gospel, you are guilty of much resistance and opposition to the Spirit of God. The dispensation of the gospel is called by the apostle, "the ministration of the Spirit," (2 Cor. 3:8). There are few, if any, who live to an age of understanding, but they are often found under the strivings of the Spirit, causing them to see their sin and danger, and putting them in mind of the necessity of Christ, of faith, and of repentance. Some yield to these motions of the Spirit. But these that neglect the salvation offered them, refusing the Holy Spirit in his attempts to persuade them to Christ, become guilty of sinning against more grace and love. They may feel a divine power going along with the word, by which it sensibly touches their consciences, convinces of sin, and in God's name condemns for it. They are urged to repentance and faith in Christ to obtain peace and pardon with God. And yet they resist. Now how tremendous a consideration is this, that you should be guilty of resisting the Holy Spirit, withstanding the methods of divine grace to save you? If you slight the favor of God and make a light account of the blood of Christ, disregard the promises and despise the threatening of the gospel, and resist the Spirit of God in its application of them, how inexcusable will you be?

USE III. Consider this warning to all who have neglected the great salvation offered you in the gospel, to no longer persist in your neglect of it. You have done so too long already; there's no just apology or plea that you can make for your delay, and you will render your case the *worse* by persisting in a thing so sinful and unreasonable. None of you will defend the obstinacy of the Jews that had the first offer of gospel grace but neglected and refused it. So why will you imitate their practice, continuing to be reckless with your own souls and provoke God to exclude you as he has them? It is your privilege at present to enjoy the light of the gospel; with all clarity and liberty the best mercies are freely offered to you. God justly expects that his offers are received thankfully, however, and that you are not distracted by your worldly interests from securing heavenly and eternal mercies. It will be the saddest of consequences if after such opportunities and encouragements you fail to obtain eternal life. How stinging will be the reproaches of conscience for it? To enforce this matter,

Consider 1. The greatness of this sin of unbelief in rejecting Christ and the salvation that he offers. It is not without cause that God has so often assigned damnation to it and so plainly threatened the ruin of those that continue in it. Too often this sin is looked upon as a small matter, and yet this sin is very sinful. It may appear that this sin flows from the wickedness of men's hearts, as all other sins do. However, it rather flows from the blindness of men's minds and the many unworthy thoughts of God that they are ready to entertain. They doubt his wisdom, his holiness, and his truth. They are more ready to believe the word of a man than the word of God. Unbelief reflects upon the truth and faithfulness of God. Here it is said in 1 John 5:10, "He that believes not God has made him a liar." How fearful a thing is it to reproach the God of truth, one that cannot lie? It virtually denies the sufficiency of Christ, as if he were not a fit object of trust, not the all-sufficient and complete Savior God testifies him to be that is able to save to the uttermost them that come to God by him. It disparages the wisdom of God, as if he had provided a way of salvation for men that had no need of. It is a sin that is rooted in the pride, perverseness, and obstinacy of men's hearts. Therefore Christ said to them in John 5:40, "You will not come to me that you may have life." This is a sin committed against more grace, mercy, and love than many other sins are. In this way it is said to be the damning sin, the sin that binds the guilt of all other sins upon the soul and cuts it off from the last and only remedy.

Consider 2. What misery this sin of neglecting the great salvation offered by Christ has brought upon others. If we only look into the state of the Jews, their example is very instructive and awakening. The apostle tells us in Romans 11:20, that, "for unbelief they were broken off." Their sin was exceedingly great because they crucified the prince of life, the very Son of God. But it pleased God to make them the offer of salvation that was purchased by that precious blood afterward, and had they received the offer, it would have been effectual in forgiving them that sin. But for their unbelief God rejected them. They were once a people highly favored by God; there was no other people in the world for many generations so privileged by God as they were, but now as the apostle tells us that wrath is come upon them to *the uttermost* (1 Thess. 2:16). None of their privileges could protect them from such an astonishing desolation. Historians observe this as remarkable in their desolation, that God picked one of the most merciful emperors that ever swayed the Roman scepter to be the instrument of it, that their destruction might appear to be from the hand of heaven rather than from the cruelty of man. And yet very dismal was their desolation, in that eleven hundred thousand are said to have perished by the sword and famine, and ninety thousand were sold for slaves. So, if God did not spare the natural branches as the apostle argues, others have no reason to be high-minded that he will spare them; for hell is the place and portion of unbelievers.

Consider 3. How incapable you are to perform any act of duty to God, or to find acceptance with God in any service you perform, unless and until you are interested in this salvation by faith in Christ and a saving conversion to God. It is only in the name and upon the account of Christ that our persons and services come to be of any account with God. Without Christ, God is a consuming fire, ready to consume and destroy all the works and workers of iniquity. The *covenant of works* accepts no obedience but that of a holy person, free from all imperfection. And you have no claim by the *covenant of grace* until you consent to its terms. If therefore you are not united to Christ by faith, and you do not have the spirit of holiness enlivening you, then you can't plead acceptance in anything that you do. God takes no pleasure in those who will not be rewarded or crowned by God at last. Therefore the very praying as well as the plowing of the wicked is sin.

Consider 4. Think how uncertain your opportunity of obtaining the salvation that the gospel offers may be. God has long been offering the blessings of the gospel to you; but he has limits to his patience and determines how long it will be exercised, not only towards men in general but towards particular people. And you do not know the limits God has set to it, nor when you shall come to the end of it. People of all ranks and ages often go suddenly to the grave. They who expect to have a lot of years ahead of them, find themselves being summoned by death as this man in Luke 12:21 did, "This night thy soul shall be required of thee." And 1 Thessalonians 5:3 describes a similar situation, "when they cry peace and safety, sudden destruction as travail upon a woman with child, seizes upon them." Getting out of a state of sin into a state of grace and salvation is a work of great difficulty and ordinarily will require time. Your own corruptions will rise in opposition against it. Further Satan will do all he can to divert and discourage you. Therefore, if you neglect this offer of salvation, rivers of tears throughout the ages of eternity will not do that for you which the blood of Christ applied by faith is able to do right now to atone the wrath of a sin-revenging God. Cry mightily to God for the convincing, humbling, and converting power of his Spirit. Yield a present obedience to the motions of the spirit upon your hearts, whether by the word or providences of God.

Listen to no thoughts of delay or presumptions of future time and grace. This will give hope that your souls shall live and not die.

USE IV. In conclusion, to all that have professed to embrace and receive the great salvation that has been offered in the gospel and are waiting for the full accomplishment of it, this is to exhort you to make it your concern to answer the great design of God and to walk worthy of your privilege. Christians need arguments of terror as well as of comfort and hope to bind them to their duty. The apostle felt the constraining power of the love of Christ (2 Cor. 5:14) and was careful of his duty upon that ground. At the same time, the terrors of the Lord had an influence upon him (ver. 11). The certain and inexpressible misery of those who neglect this great salvation should be a powerful inducement to all who profess to hope for the blessings of it, to walk and live so that they may never come short of it. We are acquainted with the great design of the redeemer and the duty of the redeemed (Titus 2:11-14). Would God be at the expense of such wisdom, grace, and love that he might restore sinful man to his favor and image and design him to be a partaker of an inheritance in heaven, and not manage this design in a way suitable to his own holiness? Would the blessed Jesus submit to such suffering and afterward allow his people to live however they please? Would the Holy Spirit dispense his grace to sinners in their conversion and sanctification, and not expect a due application of the principles implanted in them? The apostle speaks plainly to both of these in 2 Corinthians 5:15, "If one died for all then were all dead, that they that live should not henceforth live to themselves but to him that died for them." And Galatians 4:25, "If you live in the spirit, see that you walk in the Spirit." The grace shed abroad in your hearts by the Spirit should appear in your lives as the genuine effect of the grace and spirit of Christ's work upon your hearts. In sum, your great duty is to adorn the gospel, to live as to show that you do indeed believe the promises and love the precepts of it. Be exhorted to these two things,

1. To a daily exercise of faith in the Lord Jesus Christ. The *covenant of grace* contains the promises of all things needful for this life and that which is to come. As in Colossians 1:19 and 1 Corinthians 1:30, God will have all men honor the son, as they honor the Father. One means of doing this is by their dependance upon him, by coming to God in his name and worthiness for all the blessings they stand in need of.

Let it be your concern then to trust the Lord Jesus Christ for your preservation in a state of justification and for the comfort of it. Holiness in the people of God is incomplete. Corruption is still in place, as the flesh still wars against the spirit. Sin will break through, giving Satan advantage to bring in accusations against you and stir up fears of whether you can truly obtain pardon from God. Now at the same time you should run to God in penitent confession of sin. It is your duty to renew faith in the Lord Jesus Christ for pardoning mercy as we read in Romans 1:17, that, "the righteousness of God is revealed from faith to faith." As faith brings a sinner into a justified estate, so by faith he is preserved in it. God directs us in 1 John 2:1, "If any man sin, we have an advocate with the Father Jesus Christ the righteous, and he is the propitiation for our sins." It is the duty of believers to guard against a self-righteous spirit, and not to expect their pardon upon account of their sorrows for present guilt, past services, or future purposes of better obedience. But to remember that it is by the righteousness of Christ that they are at first brought into a justified estate, so by his continual intercession for them they are continued in it, working to honor Christ by renewed acts of faith.

Again, exercise faith in the Lord Jesus Christ for your preservation and progress in a state of sanctification. This is another principal part of our salvation, and it is derived from Christ who is said to be made of God for sanctification. He that is acquainted with the holiness of God and the sinfulness and wretchedness of his own heart will see the need for a greater power than his own for the preservation and increase of grace in his own soul. God has graciously provided for the help of his people in Christ for the carrying on of this work (Eph. 5:26). And you must honor Christ by believing the promises he has made to that end such as these, Ezekiel 36:26-27, Micah 7:19, and Hebrews 8:10 by exercising and applying the means he appointed for it – the word, sacraments, and prayer, and by enforcing the precepts he gave for it, as well as a dependance on him in all your conflicts and temptations and for strength and assistance in all duties and services. In this way Christ promotes holiness and cherishes grace in the hearts of his people, to make his power glorious in their weakness and to give them cause to say with the apostle in Philippians 4:13, "I can do all things through Christ who strengthens me."

Again, exercise faith in a dependance upon Christ for acceptance of your persons and services with God. Believers often have low thoughts of themselves and of the services they do for God, and well they should, considering our sinful state. But this often leads to discouragements and doubts that God will disapprove of them. But under the deepest concerns of your own unworthiness, it benefits you to entertain honorable thoughts of the worthiness of Christ and to behold the human nature that God exalted in him, to see God well pleased with him. Also, Paul reminds us in Ephesians 1:6, that "we are accepted in the beloved." Consider the fulness of his satisfaction and the prevalence of his intercession, who as the great high priest entered into the heavens for us (Heb. 6:20). He bears the names of his people upon his breast, presents their persons and services before God, atones for their defects, and clothes them with his merit. Understanding the mediatory work of Christ will lift up your drooping spirits.

Again, exercise faith in the Lord Jesus Christ with respect to your expectations of future glory and immortality. It is unfortunate that not only the greatest number of those who live in the common light of Christianity are blinded to spiritual things, governed by sense and appetite, and crave only pleasure, profit, and honor rather than consider eternity to which they are hastening. They are much more impressed with temporal advantages than they are with the hopes of eternal mercies. This greatly dishonors Christ. But to others these things are real. These are looking for the blessed hope (Titus 2:14), for a city that has foundations (Heb. 11:10). And while reflecting on the greatness of it, these are ready with trembling hearts to say, "who shall ascend the hill of the lord, and stand in his holy place?" As explained in Ephesians 1:14, Christ Jesus paid the price of heaven for his people and fulfilled the condition of eternal life in his perfect obedience to the law. He carried our nature into heaven and took possession of it as a forerunner and surety for his people. May this truth comfort your hearts in the expectation that heaven itself, as great and as rich an inheritance as it is, is not a greater gift than Christ is. We may therefore conclude with the apostle in Romans 8:32 that as "He spared not his own Son, but delivered him up for us all, how shall he not with him freely give us all things?" But it is not in these only, but in all conditions of life, in all temptations and trials, it is your duty and will be your comfort to continually exercise your faith in the Lord Jesus Christ.

2. Be exhorted to a life of universal obedience and holy walking before God. The apostle tells us in Hebrews 5:9 that "he has become the author of eternal salvation to all of them that obey him." Christ is a king and lawgiver as well as a Savior to his people. It is his aim to make them holy as well as happy. Indeed, this ought to be looked upon as a main part of our happiness, as well as the way leading to it. And there is no sincere choice of Christ and subjection to him, where he is not received as a *King* as well as *Savior*. It is

an abuse of the grace of Christ manifested in the gospel when men presume that they themselves can continue in sin without due consequence. Christ by suffering for sin has given us the clearest representation of the evil nature of sin and its extreme offensiveness to God. By the holiness of his life, he has given us the most excellent pattern of obedience, and by the purity of his laws he shows us the most perfect rule of obedience. All these clearly show what he expects from his people. The great duty of the gospel is love, and love for Christ is especially to be expressed by obedience as in that precept of Christ in John 14:15, "If ye love me keep my commandments." And that this is the most clear and genuine fruit of love, Christ further declares in verses 21:23-24. God's love to us is a love of beneficence, but our love to him is a love of reverence and obedience, a love to please and honor him. As 1 John 5:3 declares, "This is the love of God that we keep his commandments. And his commandments are not grievous." And 1 Peter 1:15, "But as he which hath called you is holy, so be ye holy in all manner of conversation." Here God himself is proposed as a pattern, which shows that the highest measures of holiness should be the aim of Christians; they should make it their design to resemble the God they worship. It honors God when his people are witnesses to his holiness, when they testify to the holiness of God in his nature and laws by the holiness of their walk. God being perfectly holy both in respect to the purity of his essence and the integrity of his administrations, shows that Christians should also be holy in the state and attitude of their souls as well as in their actions and general behaviors. Not only our religious, but also our civil actions, ought to be done to honor God and for his glory. In every condition of life, holiness should appear. When surrounded with blessings, our heart should be filled with thankful praises to God; and we should be ready to serve him with joyfulness and gladness of heart in the abundance of all things that he gives. Under afflictions we should be holy, bringing forth fruits of repentance, meekness, patience, and a due resignation to his divine will. And in every relation – husbands and wives, parents, masters, children, and servants – the holiness of Christians should shine forth in a conscientious observation of all behavior relative to our duties, toward families as well as neighbors. We render our holiness questionable when it doesn't show up in their relationships as this is the principal sphere of our activity. Therefore, it is here that we have the most frequent occasions to express it. And a course of holiness in all relative duties will have an extensive influence upon others, who shall be better for it, and will hopefully be ready to imitate it, or at least be awed by it. Indeed, if piety isn't carefully maintained in families, it will lessened everywhere else.

You have another precept in Luke 1:74-75, where our duty is made the end of our deliverance. Christ came not to exempt us from the service of God, but that we might serve him without servile fear and with cheerfulness and joy of heart. And the branches of duty here urged are holiness and righteousness. The former includes a holy fear of, faith in, and love to God as our highest good, our portion and blessedness as well as a reverence of his name, both in our thoughts and expressions. We have to do with God who is glorious in holiness, and we will be sanctified by drawing near to him. Not only does he observe all our actions, but he also knows the most secret motions and workings of our hearts. Righteousness has to do with our duties owed to men, according to the relationships we have with them, or they with us. We owe respect and honor to superiors, and it is a matter of justice to yield it to them. We owe respect and love to all men and must be careful not to injure them in any way. We are to model holiness to them, in words and practice, avoiding all obscenity in words and gestures. According to that precept in 1 Thessalonians 4:6, there must be no unfairness in our dealings one with another and no unfaithfulness in our promises. Again, no injury must be done to the names of others, by receiving or spreading defamations. See that you are charitable towards all men, ready to vindicate them wherever there is need of it and ground for it. Christ came not to make the law void but rather to explain and enforce it, that he might render holiness more evident and raise his people to greater exercise in it than ever before. And it should be the aim and design of all Christians, for Christ's sake as well as their own and others, that their graces may be resplendent in the holiness and universal righteousness that as the apostle directs, "they may adorn the gospel," (Titus 2:10), and walk worthy of their relationship to God (Col. 1:10). Their present privileges are from him (Heb. 12:28, 1 Peter 2:5) as well as their future hopes (1 Cor. 15:58). This will do more to recover

Part 5

and maintain the honor of Christianity, and of the God and Savior that Christians profess than their highest eulogies or praises.

FINIS.

The Serious Consideration that God Will Visit and Judge Men for Sin[4]

A Sermon on Serious Thoughts on Restraining from Sin

Job 31:14, "What then shall I do when God rises up? and when he visits, what shall I answer him?"

Being assembled here on such a solemn occasion of one of our own under a sentence of death for crimes committed, it is very fit that it should be accompanied with the word of God and prayer. When such a large audience of Christians are brought together in a serious mindset to consider the sorrowful effects of sin and how soon they go down to the grave for it, we trust that they, as well as the one sentenced, may receive some divine instruction.

And having been asked by the reverend pastor of the church in this town to stand in his place on this occasion, I have turned my thoughts on this serious subject: the words which I have now read to you and that we should always be in awe of so that *we do not sin against God*. This is the application we should make of these instances of judgment

---

[4] A sermon preached at Cambridge, September 15, 1738, on occasion of the execution of Philip Kennison, for the crime of burglary. By William Williams, MA. Ezek. 18:20-21, "The wickedness of the wicked shall be upon him. But if the wicked turn from all his sins, he shall surely live." Deut. 13:11, "And all Israel shall hear and fear, and do no more any such wickedness." With the Confession of his Faith. (Boston, MA: Printed and sold by Thomas Fleet), 1738.

executed upon men for their sin, and of the admonitions and warnings of the word, whereas the wrath of God is revealed from heaven against the ungodliness and unrighteousness of men.

In this chapter, which is the conclusion of Job's discourse with his friends, he makes a very significant and solemn defense of his innocence and integrity, and that he was clear of the crimes that his friends either charged him with or might suppose him to be guilty of. This defense was not done in a spirit of pride or self-righteousness but rather was a just and necessary vindication of himself. "Happy is the man whose heart is upright towards God!" He considered God as his judge, as well as his creator (v. 15). And therefore, he would not do any unrighteous thing to his fellow man because of this supposition: "what if I should do so, what then should I do if God rises up against me?" for God is so superior to me and all men in infinite power and inflexible justice!

In this and many other passages in the chapter, Job shows that he shuns evil because he had a devout regard for God and a reverential fear of him, in that his righteousness was the foundation for his justice and charity.

To give some explanation of the words:

"When God rises up…" Such postures of sitting and rising are often attributed to God in Scripture, but only figuratively, or after our manner of speaking. God is said to sit on his throne, in allusion to earthly princes and judges who sit and hear causes and give sentence. Therefore, he may be said to rise up when he proceeds to execute judgment. To rise up notes "readiness to speech or action". God's "rising up" indicates the manifestation of his purpose and the execution of his power. Moses prays in Numbers 10:35, "Rise up, Lord, and let thine enemies be scattered." His church is also taught to pray this way in Psalm 68:1. When men expose themselves to God's displeasure by sin, they have reason to put this frightful question to themselves, "what shall I do when God rises up?" The expression suggests either one asking counsel and advice, not knowing what to do, or it signifies in the language of grief and trouble, one who is perplexed with the realization of what he has done and the fear of what he shall suffer as a result.

"And when he visits, what shall I answer him?"

To visit is, in the scriptural sense, sometimes to show favor and kindness. Luke 1:68 is an example, "God has visited and redeemed his people."

But that is not what is meant in our text.

"To visit" can also mean "to manifest displeasure, and to execute judgment," As Exodus 32:34 notes, "Nevertheless, in the day when I visit, I will visit their sin upon them." In other words, by way of punishment, they shall suffer the sorrowful effects of their sin (see also Jer. 5:9).

Further, "to visit" can also signify to call to an account. This is the privilege of a superior toward those under his charge and inspection (Hos. 4:9).

In our text, both the second and third cases are relevant. And by asking the question, the writer is concerned that he should not be able to answer when God should call him to account for contemptuous treatment or unrighteousness of his fellow man. He realizes that he could not excuse himself, nor could he expect to escape God's righteous judgment.

These are very weighty questions which we should keep close to our heart as a proper means to prevent sinning: "What shall I do when God rises up? And when he visits, what shall I answer him?"

The serious consideration of God's visiting and judging us for our sins would be an effective means to prevent us from sinning against him.

In the 23rd verse of this chapter, Job likewise professes "destruction from God was a terror to me!" Well may it be so, it is so to nature, and it is so to a gracious soul. Some avoid evil and sin for fear of punishment only. This is a servile fear. But there is also a filial fear, which should be sought after and cherished. This sanctified affection is tempered with love for God and does not inflict the soul with fear but rather keeps it from wandering from the path of righteousness.

Often men don't consider that they are afraid of the judgments of God. This lack of consideration is the great misery of men! They don't even *consider* that they do evil. And therefore, neither do they consider the consequences of doing evil. They omit the duties God requires of them and transgress his sacred laws. Divine counsels and persuasions cannot move such men to any good purpose, because they do not allow themselves to ponder and consider. This is

God's complaint of his people in Isaiah 1:3, "Israel does not know, my people do not consider."

There are very weighty considerations which God sets before men in order that they might not dare sin against him. These considerations are sufficient to dissuade their corrupt inclinations and the strongest temptations which they are exposed to. But they will not apply their hearts to these thoughts. It would surely be a very powerful tendency to prevent men's sinning if they would seriously consider what they should do when God "rises up and visits" them.

This may be evident, if we consider the following topics.

1. That such thoughts will lead them to consider that their time of probation will at some point come to an end. There will certainly be an end of their time and manner of life. God has placed men here on earth in a state of trial for eternity. They have a great business to do, and but a short time in which to do it. There is a time and season for every lawful business that men must carry out. If they would consider, surely, they must conclude that God in whose hands their breath is, and whose are all their ways, will bring their opportunities to an end, and that they do not know how soon. He will not wait always, and it may be not long. A few weeks or days, or for what they know, one more hour may bring them to an end. God will not always be still and silent; he will put an end to all their worldly enjoyments and pursuits, all their sensual gratifications, all their sports and pleasures, and above all, all their opportunities to seek the favor of God and make provision for their souls.

2. This should lead them to consider that a righteous God will call them to account for all that they do. This is the meaning of our verse, "when God rises up, and when he visits." This may refer to three distinct periods.

(1.) God often in this life reckons with men, or manifest his displeasure for their sins, in his providence upon them. In this way, "The Lord is known by the judgments which he executes," (Psa. 9:16). He said concerning his people in Jeremiah 5:9, "Shall I not visit for these things?" And Jeremiah 14:10, "I will remember their iniquity, and visit their sin," (Jer. 14:10, Hosea 9:9). Sometimes he visits them in wrath and sometimes in mercy to reduce them from the error of their ways (Psa. 89:32). He uses a variety of methods by which he visits and chastises them for their sins in this life (Lev. 26:14-39). He brings wars, scarcity, famine, and sometimes mortal sickness, all to vindicate his own name and honor, because men would not consider their ways and turn from their sins.

(2.) God visits all men at the day of death, sometimes by the hand of human justice and sometimes by his own immediate hand. It may be suitable on this occasion to mention such crimes as the laws of this land have determined to be punishable by death, as this may prevent some persons sinning in ignorance of their danger. One example is the murdering of any person, punishable by death, not only by the laws of God but also by the laws of all civilized nations. Other examples are treason of any kind, assault and robbery, burglary, breaking and entering, or any other felony one is convicted of.

The Danger of Not Reforming Known Evils

Whether by the hand of justice or the providence of God, a visit to every unrighteous man and every impenitent sinner to execute his due punishment shall be given him (Isa. 3:11). We are assured concerning men in common in Hebrews 9:27 that "It is appointed unto men once to die, and after that the judgment." Though we do not know the manner of death, yet we are sufficiently assured from many passages of Scripture that every person's judgment is passed at death, and their state irreversibly determined by the glorious Judge. The spirits of the just are made perfect, and the souls of the wicked are presently sent into the place of torments (Prov. 14:32).

(3.) The great judge will come to visit and call all men to an account at the resurrection of the dead. This we are plainly assured of in the sacred oracles, that God shall judge both the righteous and the wicked. God has appointed a day in which he will judge the world in righteousness (Acts 17:31). No man shall escape this judgment of God. We must *all* appear before the judgment seat of Christ (2 Cor. 5:10). Then the books shall be opened, and all that have lived and died from Adam to the end of time, shall be *judged* out of them (Rev. 20:12). This was what the world was warned of so long ago as in the days of Enoch (Jude 1:14-15). Thus, there will be a strict account taken as to what rules they have transgressed, what bonds and obligations they have violated, what evils they have done, and what duties they have left undone. Then sinners must stand before the vast multitude, however reluctant, miserable, and ashamed they may be! They shall be called to account for how they have used what God gave them; whether they honored the Lord with their substance and were just and honest in all their dealings and concerns with men. They will be required to give an account of whether they were merciful, kind, and charitable, and how they governed their behaviors, whether they were sober, chaste, and temperate, and whether they were good and faithful in their relationships with others. They will have to give account of how they used their time, and especially their seasons of grace, their sabbaths, and the instructions they received, and whether they made Christianity their main business. We are taught in Ecclesiastes 12:14 that God shall bring into judgment every work with every secret thing, whether it be good or evil. Then the Lord who is a God of knowledge, and by whom actions are weighed (1 Sam. 2:3), and who knows all hearts, will not only discover who and what was good and what was bad, but how good and how bad everything was that was done by men.

 And in this great audit, this visitation day, who will be able to answer? We are assured that the ungodly shall not stand in the judgment. The Lord acknowledges the way of the righteous; only those who have had a work of holiness wrought in them and the righteousness of Christ imputed to them will be saved.

 Would not such thoughts closely pressed upon the mind, restrain us from all sin and promote our repentance?

 3. By such thoughts they would be able to discern the vanity and insufficiency of their pleas and excuses used to quiet themselves in their sinful neglects and transgressions.

Sometimes we excuse our sin by saying that we were drawn into sin by ensnaring companions. But if we consider that God takes notice of our sins, and will rise up against them in displeasure, not allowing our iniquity to go unpunished, would this knowledge not be more powerful to restrain us than any enticements could be to allure us? Surely, we would rather listen to the wisdom of Proverbs 1:10, "My son, if sinners entice thee, consent thou not."

What temptations of honor, worldly gains, or sensual pleasure can be of equal force with these considerations? Which would convince men that to sin against God is to wrong their own souls and practically choose death! And what is the honor that is gained by sin? Superficial and vanishing and which will end in shame and everlasting contempt! What is that pleasure worth, or how dear is it bought near, which is but short lived and will end in bitterness and everlasting pain? And what are the gains of unrighteousness and fraud, stealth, and robbery, which bring a curse from God, and for which the righteous judge shall cast them into the prison of hell? As Romans 6:21 warns, "What fruit had ye then of those things whereof ye are now ashamed? For the end of those things is death." And Matthew 16:26, "What is a man profited, if he shall gain the whole world, and lose his own soul?"

Some are tempted to dismiss serious thoughts as uncomfortable and melancholy, or if they have some concern about forsaking their sins and turning to God, they stumble at the difficulties of repentance and conversion.

But would not these thoughts convince men that it will be far more difficult to bear the displeasure and wrath of an angry God?

Would not the thoughts of God's anger, and the realization that they must stand before his dread tribunal, make them use their greatest efforts to cry to him for pity and help?

Would they flatter themselves with purposes of repentance hereafter, and live careless in their delays? Surely these thoughts closely applied would wake them up to the truth. If they considered that God is angry with the wicked every day, and his judgments may at any moment be brought against them and death overtake them; they would not dare to boast of tomorrow, when they do not know what a day may bring forth; but today they would hear his voice and not harden their hearts.

These solemn thoughts would serve to dismiss all vain pleas and excuses by which men too often solace themselves in their negligence and lack of repentance.

4. Lastly, these thoughts would naturally lead them to understand something of the greatness and dreadfulness of the punishment which God will inflict upon sinners. Our Lord has warned us what the terrible sentence will be that is pronounced upon sinners in the great day (Matt. 25:41). And after that the punishment which will follow (ver. 46). This punishment will fall upon both body and soul as noted in Matthew 16:28, "fear him who can destroy both body and soul in hell," and Mark 9:44, "where the worm does not die and the fire is not quenched."

The misery that is depicted in Scripture is described by the most awful distressing and afflicting things in nature, so that we might know that nothing can fully represent the dreadfulness of the wrath of God. Their pains will far exceed all the pains and miseries in this world! As Matthew 16:42 notes, "... shall cast them into a furnace of fire, where there shall be weeping and gnashing of teeth!"

They will not know how to bear the torment, neither can they in any way shun or escape it; and the everlasting duration adds to the devastation of it. There will be no intermission of their misery, no end, as it will abide forever!

If sinners would seriously consider these things, would they not admit that it is a fearful thing to fall into the hands of the living God? (Heb. 10:31). And would not such reflections make them afraid to offend him and convince them that it is the extremity of folly and madness, for the sake of the temporary gains or pleasures of sin, to expose themselves to such tremendous evils!

USE 1. We learn that they are very foolish who do not take it into serious consideration that God will visit them for their sins or bring them into judgment; yet we have reason to think that there are many who, though they bear the name of Christians and profess to own the truths of the gospel, still neglect this great business of life and go on in their sins.

Some are pursuing earthly things, and their worldly affections direct their thoughts to seek after such objects. Some make provision for the flesh to fulfil their lusts and are indulging their sensual inclinations. Some have secret hopes that there is no occasion for such thoughts, and flatter themselves that they shall have peace (Deut. 29:19). Some are afraid to entertain such serious thoughts and strive to divert them because they dampen their spirits and render their pleasures boring and make their enjoyments gloomy. But let it be known that all those who despise God's authority and government greatly injure their own souls.

To all who are yet impenitent, who indulge themselves in sinful practices, let me persuade you to put these questions to yourselves, now and often, "what shall I do when God rises up? And when he visits, what shall I answer him?" Can you conceive of God himself putting this solemn question to you? If he did, could your heart endure? "Could your hands be strong in the days that I shall deal with thee?" (Ezek. 22:14).

1. What will you do if God shall deal with you in a *judicial* way, and visit you with some distressing temporal judgment? This is not uncommon. Divine providence visits men with temporal evils and calamities. Many sorts of sins, and particularly pride, God especially hates. As Proverbs 29:23 says, "A man's pride shall bring him low," and Proverbs 16:18, "Pride goes before destruction, and a haughty spirit before a fall." God will also punish uncleanness (Heb. 13:4), adulterers (Eph. 5:6), intemperance (Prov. 23:21). The drunkard and the glutton shall come to poverty. Proverbs 23:29-30 warns, "Who hath woe? who hath sorrow? who hath contentions? who hath babbling? who hath wounds without cause? who hath redness of eyes? They that tarry long at the wine; they that go to seek mixed wine." He often

threatens unrighteousness and oppression. As in Ezekiel 22:13, "I have smitten my hand at thy dishonest gain." And Proverbs 21:7, "The robbery of the wicked shall destroy them." It brings temporal evils and calamities as well as exposes to future destruction. What will you do when your sins have brought such evils upon you? What will comfort you? Will the gain be worth the loss?

And even those who avoid these blatant sins may be liable to suffer the judgments of God. The apostle warned the Corinthians against sinful disorder and irreverence and said that "many are weak and sickly among you, and many fallen asleep," because of it (1 Cor. 11:30).

God is yet threatening us. Should we not take the warning, and put that solemn question to ourselves, "what will you do in the day of visitation? To whom will ye flee for help?" (Isa. 10:3). If his visitation should reach us, as it has many others, why should we expect exemption? What will you do when you see death suddenly seizing your tender offspring, your beloved children, and threatening yourselves? To whom will you flee for help? You may run for help from your friends and neighbors, or from the physician, but all help will fail if God does not help you. Will you not then repent of your sins, by which you have displeased the Lord? Why not now renounce them and get into a state of reconciliation with God so that you may not have the terrors of an accusing conscience to grapple with, besides the afflicting strokes of God's hand!

2. What will you do in the day of death? When the Lord of life sends the king of terrors to visit you? And the time will certainly and may speedily come!

When your opportunities are at an end, what will you do? When you say, "I shall go to the gates of the grave," will you not look back on your past seasons with grief and bitterness? To think how God has called and you refused, and that he may now justly refuse to hear your cry? You may wish earnestly for more time, but in vain. You may now think yourselves secure, and that you may continue to live in ease and pleasure. But what will you do for your neglected soul when that awful hour is upon you, your strength and spirits are failing and you find yourself gasping for breath, expecting to receive your doom? Oh, how will your heart fail you, what distress and anguish will seize you!

3. Lastly, what will you do in that great and terrible day of the Lord? When he comes to judgment, what will you answer him if you die in your sins?

When you shall see the Son of God coming in his glory, and with the glory of the Father and all the holy angels! (Matt. 25:31). When he shall make his last visit to this earth, to determine the state of every man according to his works, will not your heart and flesh tremble to think how you have slighted and despised him? Will you remember how you refused his most gracious offers and would not obey his most reasonable commands? O how terrible to have your only Savior become your *enemy*? To whom can you flee for help then? We are told in Revelation 1:7, "Behold he cometh with clouds, and every eye shall see him, and they also who pierced him, and all kindreds of the earth shall wail because of him!"

And what will you do, how will you bear it, when you shall see the saints at his right hand in robes of glory? (Matt. 25:33). And some perhaps, that have been your relatives or acquaintances in this world, to think that you had the same opportunities and advantages and offers of life that they had, but indulged your sin and, alas, lost your soul! (Luke 13:28). There shall be weeping and gnashing of teeth when you see Abraham and Isaac and Jacob in the kingdom of God, and you yourselves thrown out!

And when the all-knowing Judge shall bring all your sins to your remembrance, and set them in order before your eyes, what will you do? How will you answer him? When conscience will witness against you for all you have done as well as all those duties you have left undone! Whatever pleas and excuses sinners comfort themselves with now, they will have no excuse for their sin then. All those who have enjoyed the gospel, and yet are found without the wedding garment of righteousness and holiness, will then be speechless (Matt. 22:12).

And what will you do when you hear the dreadful sentence pronounced from the glorious judge, as the last word to the wicked (Matt. 25:41), "Depart ye cursed, into everlasting fire, prepared for the devil and his angels!" O! what unutterable horror, confusion, and anguish will fill your souls!

And when presently the tremendous doom is executed upon you, with what despair will you cry out, "what shall I do?" How will you be able to bear the loss of all good? How will you be able to endure the suffering of all evil? When you have no friend to support you, and no hope to relieve or comfort you forever, how will you bear it?

Those who seriously consider these things now and call their souls into account, would surely resolve by the strength of Christ to forsake sin and attend their duty, and earnestly endeavor to gain reconciliation with God, or else they must be stupid and hardened and not afraid of the wrath of the Almighty!

I urge you to call your sins to remembrance and let your most earnest inquiry be, "What shall I do? How shall I answer my judge for my many and heinous sins?" And be heartily concerned to take the right course.

May you call to mind the pertinent admonitions and counsels which have been given you. Be very thankful for the kind assistances you have had. I earnestly entreat you, look deeply into your heart, and beware that you don't deceive yourself. Pray to God, "where I do not see, teach me. Let me discern if there is any wickedness in my heart, and lead me in the way everlasting."

Don't depend upon any external privilege or ordinance as if grace and salvation were necessarily connected. Rather examine and see whether you find your heart turned from sin to God. If you have had sorrow and heaviness for your sins, consider whether you have had a right understanding of the glorious excellencies of God against whom you have sinned. Do you mourn that you have despised the rightful authority of your Creator and

Lawgiver, and abused his mercy and goodness which should have led you to repentance? Are you sorrowful that you have undervalued and slighted so often the grace of a most compassionate redeemer, who came to bless us by turning us from all our iniquities! Do these and such considerations melt your heart, making you realize that it is an evil thing that you have forsaken the Lord, and that his fear has not been in your heart?

Have you been brought to see yourself in a spiritual sense, as a poor helpless, wretched, undone creature; and that you can make no amends, no satisfaction to divine justice for your offences by your prayers or tears or promises? Do you realize that you are a prisoner of hope? You have read and heard that this is a faithful saying, and worthy of all acceptance, *that Jesus Christ came into the world to save sinners*, even the chief. How did you receive this good news of the gospel?

Do you indeed believe that Jesus is the Christ, the Son of the living God? And that as a glorious high priest, he appears in the heavens for us and can save to the uttermost all that come unto God by him? Then do not let the magnitude of your sins discourage your coming to him in repentance, nor prevent your pleading and trusting in the infinite merits of the all-sufficient Savior. God can pardon great sins, and save the chief of sinners, consistent with the honor of his justice, holiness, and truth.

Consider that this is the work most pleasing to God that you can perform: to believe in the name of his son Jesus Christ, and put your trust in his perfect righteousness, committing your soul into his hands that he would save it from sin and from the hands of your spiritual enemies and from eternal death. You are going to appear before the Judge of all the earth! Does this fill you with dread, under a sense of your guilt, and that you have nothing to answer? Let this thought be your support, that Christ graciously offers to be your Savior, and assures you that whosoever comes to him, he will not cast out. If you can now come to him weary and heavy laden with your sins, desirous to be saved from all sin, and to be made holy and fit for the heavenly inheritance, then your estate will be safe. This miserable death will not separate you from his favor. Unbelief will damn you, but if you believe in Christ, your other sins will not.

O! may the wonderful love of Christ, who died on a tree to save us from eternal death, *draw your heart to him.*

Call to mind that memorable instance of one of the thieves that was crucified with Christ, while confessing that he was receiving the due reward of his deeds, said unto Christ, "Lord, remember me when you come into your kingdom," (Luke 23:41-42). Likewise, under a sense of your own rightful suffering, humbly look unto Jesus with this dying wish and fervent prayer, "Lord remember me now that you are exalted in your heavenly kingdom. Lord Jesus receive my spirit."

To conclude, give honor to God, as far as you can, by bearing testimony to his righteous laws and by public confession of your sins.

And give warning to others, that they may not sin against God, nor pursue any evil, wicked ways which lead to destruction! Particularly the young people, that they do not heed the temptations of Satan but rather fear God in their youth and beware of departing from God

If you are enabled by divine grace to comply with the counsels given you and are heartily desirous to give glory to God, you shall be among those in whom free grace shall be forever admired which may God grant, for his mercy's sake, in Jesus Christ. To whom be glory forever. Amen.

FINIS

Other Newly Published Works at Puritan Publications

Man's Life in Light of Eternity
by Thomas Doolittle (1632–1707)

Sparks of Divine Glory: A Practical Study of the Attributes of God
by C. Matthew McMahon

A Devotional on Our Savior's Death and Passion
by Charles Herle (1598-1659)

The Wonders of Jesus
by Jeremiah Burroughs (1599-1646)

The Great Mystery of God's Providence, and Other Works
by George Gifford (1547-1620)

5 Marks of Christian Resolve
by C. Matthew McMahon

A Biblical Guide to Hearing and Studying the Word
by Richard Greenham, et. al.

A Watchman Over Christ's Church
by C. Matthew McMahon

The Danger of Not Reforming Known Evils

Attending the Lord's Table
by Henry Tozer (1602-1650)

Discovering the Glorious Love of Christ
by John Durant (1620-1686)

God is Our Refuge and Our Strength
by George Gipps (n.d.)

God, a Rich Supply of All Good
by Nathaniel Holmes (1599–1678)

I Am for You: God's Power in Supporting His People
by C. Matthew McMahon

Reformation of the Heart, Soul and Mind
by C. Matthew McMahon

Remembering Your Creator
by Matthew Mead (1630-1699)

Repentance and Prayer
by Ralph Brownrig (1592–1659)

The Blessed God
by Daniel Burgess (1645-1713)

Other Works

The Cursed Family, or the Evil of Neglecting Family Prayer
by Thomas Risley (1630–1716)

The Excellent Name of God
by Jeremiah Burroughs (1599-1646)

The Five Principles of the Gospel
by C. Matthew McMahon

The Kingdom of Heaven is Upon You
by C. Matthew McMahon

www.ingramcontent.com/pod-product-compliance
Lightning Source LLC
Chambersburg PA
CBHW020331170426
43200CB00006B/350